Young and Unemployed

Leslie J. Francis

Costello, 1984

First published in 1984

Francis, Leslie J.
  Young and unemployed.
  1. Youth——Employment——England——London
  2. Unemployment——England——London——Psychological aspects
  I. Title
  331.3'41379421   HD6276.G73L6

ISBN 0–7104–0051–9 Cased

ISBN 0–7104–0052–7 Pbk

SB 27216 (1) £6 95. 4.85

Printed and bound in Great Britain by
Biddles Ltd, Guildford and King's Lynn

Contents

Foreword

Co-operation between London Central YMCA and the Leverhulme Trust Fund created a unique opportunity for a social psychologist to devote three years to the in-depth study of young people aged between sixteen and twenty-five years at the city centre. It was my privilege to take advantage of this opportunity. One of the issues touched on in the initial report prepared for the Leverhulme Trust Fund was the relationship between the attitudes held by young people and their experience of unemployment. At this stage I recognised that the data which I had assembled contained a much richer vein of insights into the social psychology of youth unemployment than my three year period of research had enabled me fully to explore. I am grateful to London Central YMCA and the King George's Jubilee Trust Fund for extending my contract and enabling me to produce this further study.

My aim in designing the present book was to produce an account which will be of practical interest and help to those directly involved with the problems of unemployment among young people. While including in this report enough of the theoretical background to the development of the research methodology to enable the reader to test the validity of the conclusions drawn, I have not repeated here the more detailed account of the project which is already available in the two earlier books, Youth in Transit and Experience of Adulthood, both published by the Gower Publishing Company in 1982.

London Central YMCA was responsible not only for initiating this project, but also for drawing together a body of academics from a variety of disciplines to act as a research advisory group under the chairmanship of Professor David Miller (Middlesex Hospital Medical School). Serving on this group were Professor Garth Plowman (London School of Economics), Dr Richard Farmer (Westminster Medical School), Alan Beattie (University of

London, Institute of Education), John Burrows (University of London, Extra-Mural Department), John Sutcliffe (University of Cambridge, Department of Education), together with three members of staff from London Central YMCA, Leslie Adams, Colin Mawby and Geoffrey Palmer. I am grateful to all of them for giving so generously of their time and advice.

My thanks are also due to the staff of London Central YMCA for their assistance throughout the project and for making my period with them so enjoyable and worthwhile, to the many men and women who have co-operated in the research by completing my questionnaire, to Carole Boorman for typing the orginal draft of this study, to Diana Briscoe for editorial guidance and to Clare Gowing and Judith Muskett for designing and setting the text.

Culham College Institute,   Leslie J Francis
May, 1984.

1. Introduction

Of course, unemployment can be treated as an economic problem or as a political problem, and a lot of the debate about unemployment in the 1980s is conducted at these levels. Nevertheless, underneath the economic debate and the political debate is another more fundamental set of issues. The cost of unemployment should not be calculated just in terms of the economic and political consequences, but also in terms of the social and psychological correlates.

It is a fact that unemployment is one of the major problems facing our society today. Together economic depression and technological advance have eroded, and continue to erode, the opportunities for work. In particular, it is the young who are most vulnerable. At the beginning of 1982, Britain's unemployment figures rose beyond the 3,000,000 mark. Over 1,250,000 of these 3,000,000 unemployed were under the age of twenty-five. By July 1983, the official figures for the unemployed under twenty-five years of age had risen to 1,408,000.

The purpose of this book is to turn attention away from the political and economic issues and to concentrate instead on the psychological issues. The psychology of youth unemployment remains an area which has not been adequately documented. Some considerable work was undertaken by psychologists during the great depression of the 1930s, but since the Second World War there has been until recently little incentive, need, or opportunity to stimulate this kind of psychological research.

Against this background, there are four different ways in which a social psychologist could hope to make a useful contribution to knowledge about unemployment, namely
1) the organisation of psychological theory,
2) the review of existing research reports,
3) the empirical investigation of a group of unemployed young people,
4) the comparison of the response of young people who

have experienced unemployment with those who have not.

My assessment of the current state of knowledge in the field encouraged me to opt for the fourth of these approaches. A comparative study of this nature helps us to see both the ways in which the young people who have experienced unemployment differ from those who have not, and of equal importance how they do not differ.

Setting up a comparative study is fraught with difficulties. The ideal research design would require a national sample of young people and almost limitless research funding. My own ideal was to complete the best piece of research possible on the limited resources available to me. Before examining the results of my project, it is necessary to describe with some care how it was carried out and to indicate why I have confidence in its findings.

Chapter 2, therefore, discusses the design of the project. It begins by facing the problem of gaining the co-operation of a good cross-section of sixteen to twenty-five year olds and describes how London Central YMCA provided a uniquely helpful solution to meeting young people, both those with the experience of unemployment and those without this experience. The section of this chapter on 'asking the right questions' examines the issues we decided to explore in the study and why we settled on those issues. The section on 'asking in the right way' discusses the different methods available to the research psychologist and explains why we chose the technique of closed questionniares. It also gives a clear statement of how the sample frame was organised and what the response rate was like. Finally, the section on 'asking the right people' describes in detail the 1,085 sixteen to twenty-five year olds who took part in the study and upon whom the analysis in the following chapters is based.

Chapter 3 begins the analysis by introducing the young people who have had recent experience of unemployment. On the one hand, this analysis helps us to appreciate just how widespread unemployment has now become among young people and how no clear groups of young people are thoroughly immune from this experience. On the other hand, it also serves to identify for us the groups of young people who are most vulnerable to unemployment. The chapter ends by using a sophisticated statistical technique, discriminant analysis, to test how far we can predict which young people are the most likely to have had recent experience of unemployment.

Chapters 4 through 9 examine step by step the differences between the attitudes of those who have had recent experience of unemployment and those who have not shared this experience. Each of these six chapters takes one particular set of attitudes and subjects them to close scrutiny. The six attitudinal areas are described as well-being and worry, self image and counselling, values and beliefs, morals and law, politics and society, and work and leisure.

Chapters 4 through 9 provide a great deal of detailed information into the psychological correlates of unemployment among young people. Chapter 10 then sets out to summarise this mass of detail by the use of a statistical technique known as factor analysis. The central conclusion made available by the use of factor analysis is to focus attention on two key psychological concepts: depression and radicalism. The unemployed young people are those who are most depressed with life and most radical in their disregard for the standards and mores of the society which they believe has failed them.

While the main body of this book concentrates on making generalisations about the young unemployed as a group, the final section redresses the balance by focusing carefully on a small selection of individuals. There is clearly a very real place in psychology for generalisations, but there is also the need for the corrective which helps us to appreciate the richness of each individual. Just as the earlier chapters enable us to draw conclusions about the unemployed young people in general, these character sketches remind us that the generalisations are helpful only in so far as they help us to recognise the problems which individuals face in many different ways.

2. Research Design

Tottenham Court Road tube station stands right at the centre of the London Underground network. The main line British Rail stations which link London to the rest of England, Scotland and Wales are only a few stops away. Every day people pass through here from the four corners of London, from the four corners of England, from the four corners of the world. All ages, all nationalities, all classes, meet here sixty feet underground at the centre of London. It is here that my encounter with the young unemployed at the city centre began.

As the clatter of the train disappears into the dark tunnel, a new sound begins to fill the corridor: the distorted sounds of a portable amplifier, a poorly tuned guitar and the strained notes of a female vocalist. The girl singer and the male guitarist stand with their backs partly concealing the official London Transport notice prohibiting busking. Their third male companion crouches by their feet, looking up at the rushing of passing travellers. Most of them pass by totally indifferent; a few donate a coin. London Transport staff look on with equal indifference; they have come to accept the regular infringement of the city transport's by-law.

The girl looks tired and worn. Her voice is flat and her eyes are dull. Probably she is about twenty years old. Her bearded male guitarist looks older, perhaps about twenty-five. The third member of the group seems hardly old enough to have left school. He is sixteen or seventeen and already looks totally fed up with life. What are these three young people thinking? What is it like to be their age and unemployed? What is this experience doing for the rest of their lives?

Sink into the shadows for a while and watch the faces of the travellers as they rush by. Look particularly at the young faces, those in the same age category as the young buskers, between sixteen and twenty-five. Is their attitude to life much different? What are their values, hopes and aspirations, worries and fears? How many of the young travellers are also unemployed, or still have recent memories of unemployment?

Just standing there watching, can you pick out those whose lives have been affected by unemployment: and can you begin to say what effect this experience has had? The young buskers are easy to identify, but even then you are looking in at them from the outside. What of the eighteen year old boy who left school two years ago and has never been employed, or the twenty-three year old graduate who left university only to be unemployed for the next eighteen months? What of the smartly dressed young lady who completed the secretarial course and whose only outlet for those skills has been the completion of her own job application forms, one after another?

Have you never experienced the desire to stop these young people as they emerge from the tube system into the centre of London? Have you never wanted to find out what lies behind these passing faces, what makes them tick and where the young of today think they are going? It seemed to me that this was the only sensible way to build up a true picture of the real differences between the young who have experienced unemployment and those who have not. It is not simply enough, as a number of studies have already begun to do, to study the young people who are unemployed in isolation from those who are in employment. What is needed is the opportunity to compare those who have experienced unemployment with those who have not had that experience. Nor is it simply enough to question young people about their actual experience of unemployment and work. This is only one part of their response to life. What is needed is a total and in-depth encounter with the whole of their responses to life. Only in this way is it possible to begin to tease out the deeper consequences and correlates of unemployment.

In many ways the Tottenham Court Road tube station provides an ideal setting for the researcher wishing to observe a large and random sample of young people; but what a tube station cannot do is to give the researcher the opportunity to get to know these young people in any depth. Fortunately, the precise environment I needed for the kind of work I had in mind exists only a minute's walk

away from Tottenham Court Road tube station, in Great
Russell Street: the London Central YMCA.

The new London Central YMCA, opened in 1977, was
purpose designed to provide a centre for young people at
the heart of the city. Above ground, the fifteen storey
building provides short-term hotel accommodation and
long-term hostel accommodation. At street level, there are
shops, offices, a counselling service and access to the
underground car park and conference centre. But none of
these facilities represent London Central YMCA's primary
meeting point with young people. The first three floors
below ground accommodate the Centymca Club. It is here,
within the Centymca Club, that I was able to begin to
encounter in-depth the 1,085 young people upon whom this
study of youth unemployment is based.

The London Central YMCA is an organisation with a long
history, going back to 1844, but its imaginative management
and leadership has brought the association thoroughly into
the 1980s. The Centymca Club is not just for men; it is
open to women as well. It is not just for the young; it is
open to people of all ages. It is not just for Christians; it
is open to men and women of all religious faiths and of
none. There are no young people who would not be made
to feel welcome in the Centymca Club on grounds of sex,
religion, education or social class.

The Centymca Club area has been designed to embrace a
wide range of recreational, leisure and educational
facilities. From the moment you enter the foyer a total
impression is conveyed of activity on the one hand, and
relaxation on the other. In the sports hall you may find
badminton, volley ball or basket ball taking place. Perhaps
a group is involved in circuit training, gymnastics or keep
fit exercises. An individual member may be involved in his
own personalised programme of exercises, juggling, or
learning to balance on a monocycle. At the far end, one or
two young people may be attempting to scale the brick
climbing face, and nearby a trampoline class may be in
progress. In the swimming pool there may be classes for
beginners or the subaqua club may be arranging a training
session.

Overlooking the swimming pool is the lounge area with the
coffee bar and the exhibition facilities. Groups of people
will be sitting around tables, drinking, eating, laughing,

talking. Next to the lounge area is the reading room, set aside for silent study, and off the reading room are the various classrooms, clubrooms and the chapel. There are also a range of squash courts, a second smaller sports hall, a fully equipped games room, and a professionally designed weight-training room, as well as a sauna, solarium and massage facilities.

Another set of rooms is set aside for a range of specialist programme activities: the audio studio houses the local YMCA radio station; the dark room houses the photographic club; and the print room provides the centre from which the regular newspaper is produced. The craft workshops provide facilities for a range of craft activities, do-it-yourself classes, painting and drawing classes. The lower club lounge provides facilities for the regular discos and film shows.

Both its geographical position at the centre of London, and the wide range of facilities and activities which it offers makes the Centymca Club something unique in the whole of London. In view of the breadth of what it has to offer, London Central YMCA indeed attracts a very diverse membership, making it a rich and rewarding social laboratory from which to conduct research.

ASKING THE RIGHT QUESTIONS

I started my research from the point of wanting to know how the experience of unemployment was related to the attitudes and values held by sixteen to twenty-five year olds. It was the desire to meet a random group of young people including both those who had experienced unemployment and those who had not experienced unemployment which led me to London Central YMCA. Once settled inside the Centymca Club, I faced the next problem of drawing up a conceptual map as a way of defining what I meant by looking at the attitudes of sixteen to twenty-five year olds.

I came to the conclusion that my map of attitudes should represent twelve main points of reference. This map evolved from three processes which I conducted at the same time. First, I listened to what the young members of the Centymca Club were talking about, and I engaged in wide

8

ranging conversation with a number of them myself. In this way, I became more aware of the issues they were discussing, the matters that were important to them and what they wanted to say themselves about their attitudes. At the same time, I gained an appreciation of the language the young people were using and through which I would be able to explore these matters clearly and unambiguously.

Second, I had been reading the literature both on unemployment and on the attitudes of the young. The information service at the National Youth Bureau in Leicester, friends at the University of London Institute of Education and the members of the London Central YMCA Research Advisory Group were all very helpful in enabling me to track down the relevant British, North American and European literature. The literature in the field left me discontent and convinced that as yet no one had worked out an adequate framework which I could simply take over as the basis for my own study. I decided, therefore, that it was necessary for me to make an original start and to draw up my own map.

Third, I drew upon the help of a number of professional people, both academic researchers and those more directly engaged in working with young people. What I continually asked, would these people wish to learn from a new research initiative? These conversations helped to define the precise areas within which the research could be of most practical benefit.

All three routes began to push me towards the same conclusion. It seemed to me that the important things which needed to be said about the attitudes of sixteen to twenty-five year olds could be located within a map that identified twelve key areas. The labels I chose to describe these areas are: well-being, worry, self image, counselling, values, beliefs, morals, law, politics, society, work and leisure. What I now need to do is to explain briefly what each of these labels means and how to interpret them.

Well-being

The concept of well-being is used widely in psychological research as a way of talking about the basic level of satisfaction which people feel about their lives. Like so much of the technical language used in psychological

research, the term well-being is used by different writers
with slightly different meanings, so it is important to be
clear about the way in which I am using the word. The
kind of questions I decided to ask under this heading were
general questions concerned with the young person's overall
reponse to life. More specific questions concerned with the
satisfaction they receive from individual aspects of their
lives, like their relationships, their friendships, and their
leisure time, I decided to deal with separately. Young
people who believe themselves to be experiencing a high
level of general well-being, in the sense in which I am
using the term, tend to say things like 'I find life really
worth living', or 'I feel my life has a sense of purpose'.
Young people who believe themselves to be experiencing a
low level of general well-being tend to say things like 'I am
worried that I cannot cope', 'I often feel depressed', or 'I
have sometimes considered taking my own life'.

Under this heading, I wanted to be able to work out the
relationship between the experience of unemployment and
the level of well-being enjoyed by young people. I wanted
to be able to test the extent to which the young
unemployed experience more depression than their
contemporaries who were in employment, and whether they
are at greater risk from suicidal intentions.

Worry

Listening to their conversations, the key areas of worry
which emerged from time to time are the personal ones
concerned with relationships, friendships and sex. Another
key area of worry is to do with work, or lack of work; and
related to this are worries about money matters and debts.
I also thought it important to explore the level of anxiety
among young people about their physical health and about
their mental health. I wanted to know what thought young
people gave to the risks of cancer and the problems of
growing old. I also wanted to know what proportion of
young people would claim to be worried in a general sense
about the world situation.

Some people have suggested that the unemployed become
greater worriers, not just about the things directly related
to the actual experience of unemployment itself, like work

and money, but about a whole range of other issues. I hoped to test this notion.

Self image

Self image is the term used to assess the kind of image which young people have of themselves and which they are concerned to project to others. Just like well-being, self image is a term which has come to have a wide range of meanings in the psychological literature. My intention was to use it in the specific sense of gauging the degree to which young people try to project a socially desirable image of themselves to the world at the cost of being truthful about themselves. For the purposes of this study, self image is important for two reasons.

First, a major problem in attitude research concerns the way in which people sometimes try to pull the wool over the researcher's eyes and present an untruthfully glowing picture of themselves. In this context, the self image questions act as a kind of index of untruthfulness.

Second, self image questions help us to assess how secure people feel in themselves. Some people need the support and approval of others much more deeply and urgently. They try so hard to win the support and approval of others that they cease to tell the truth about themselves. On this understanding, questions to do with self image help us to assess the way in which the experience of unemployment may threaten the confidence which young people have in themselves and the extent to which it may lead to deep feelings of insecurity.

Counselling

There is a growing awareness of the need for counselling facilities for young people, especially in the city centre. London Central YMCA, among other agencies, is responding to this need not only by providing counselling facilities within the association for residents and members, but also by opening on its premises an 'off the street' counselling service for young people in general.

There are three kinds of information I wanted to collect in the area of counselling. First, I was interested in the young people's perceptions regarding their own counselling needs and the counselling needs of their contemporaries. Second, I was interested in ascertaining the kind of people whom the young would consider approaching for counselling purposes. Third, of particular importance, I was interested in understanding more about the counselling needs of the young unemployed.

Values

Under the heading of values, I propose to look at the areas and issues to which the young person ascribes worth or importance. Three main value areas are selected for attention. These are economic values, including such notions as home ownership, making, spending and saving money; personal values, including such factors as family, friends, home, and self; and social values, including religion, morality and politics. By including these areas in the study it becomes possible to test how far fundamental values are related to the experience of unemployment.

Beliefs

Like values, beliefs are an important factor underlying the young person's response to life. I was particularly concerned to evaluate the part played by religion in the lives of young people and to assess their view of the churches. I decided to examine what they believed about God, Jesus, life after death, the church, the Bible and religious education in schools. At the same time, I wanted to examine what they believed about such things as their horoscope and the part played by luck in their lives.

Morals

What are the prevailing moral attitudes of young people in the 1980s? Do those who have experienced unemployment hold any different moral views from those who have not experienced unemployment? Under this general heading, I selected three main areas for attention: sexual ethics, including the young person's attitude towards contraception, marriage, sex outside marriage and homosexuality; the sanctity of human life, including issues like abortion, euthanasia and war; alcohol and drugs like marijuana and heroin.

Law

The purpose of this section is to identify the extent to which young people regard themselves as essentially law-abiding and the extent to which they are willing to hold aspects of the law in contempt. It also raises the question as to whether those who have experienced unemployment are any less or more law-abiding than those who have not had that experience. The kind of issues reviewed in this section include the young person's attitude towards travelling on public transport without a ticket and the evasion of tax. I also examined their attitudes towards a range of motoring offences, in particular drinking and driving.

Politics

Under this heading I decided to concentrate on three primary issues. First, I wanted to examine the young person's involvement in politics and their confidence in the policies of the major political parties. Second, I wanted to gauge their attitude on key political issues like nationalisation, education, the health service, the trade unions, immigration, the Common Market and international trade. Third, I wanted to assess their perceptions of different sectors of society by examining their attitude towards pay claims of different groups, like nurses, doctors, policemen, car workers and miners. I was interested to discover whether the experience of unemployment is related to the young person's political viewpoint.

Society

Under the concept of society, I proposed to examine the young person's attitude towards specific features of life in today's world. I wanted to assess their perceptions of current trends in such areas as the crime rate, the educational standard of schools, the efficiency of the health service, the divorce rate, the availability of abortion, violence on television, pornography and credit card facilities. At the same time, I was interested in ascertaining the extent to which they registered concern about such issues as pollution, nuclear war, the Third World, inflation, homelessness and the key issues of unemployment. How do the young unemployed feel about the society in which they live, and are their views significantly different from the young who have not experienced unemployment?

Work

I decided to look at the satisfaction which young people derive from their work, their reason for working and their ambition to do well at work. In particular, I was interested in the way in which those who had been unemployed later integrated themselves into work, and in assessing the extent to which some of the unemployed might say they preferred being unemployed to working in a job they disliked.

Leisure

The young person's attitude towards leisure is a central issue in coming to terms with unemployment. In this area, I wanted both to assess the attitude held by young people to their leisure in general and to provide a detailed picture of their preferences for different leisure time activities. How do the unemployed young people feel about their leisure time, and what do they do to occupy themselves during it? In particular I wanted to listen to what they were saying about their level of interest in the fifty or so specific activities or facilities provided within the Centymca Club. This analysis is of considerable relevance to recreation and leisure centres in developing their resources with special reference to the young and unemployed.

ASKING IN THE RIGHT WAY

The presentation of the conceptual map in the previous section has defined clearly the aims of the present study. The next problem concerns the selection of an appropriate method to achieve these aims. Given the kind of research questions which we are trying to answer, there are three basic approaches open to the research psychologist. Each of these approaches has its strengths and its weaknesses, its advantages and its disadvantages.

The first method is that of participant observation. Participant observation can open up a rich range of insights. It is, however, not ideally suited to research primarily concerned with observing underlying predispositions, like attitudes and values, which often require some kind of more in-depth probing. The other major drawback of this technique is that it places too much weight on the arbitrary selectivity of the observer. What is the observer to note as worth recording, and what is he to overlook? While I found the use of this method an essential ingredient in first setting up my study, after the initial stages I thought it wise to move on to a different and more hard nosed technique.

The second method is that of clinical interviews. This technique would involve making appointments with some of the members and interviewing them in-depth for quite some considerable time. There are three main drawbacks with the clinical interview method of research in relationship to the specific context of the project I envisage in the Centymca Club. It would be very difficult to organise a systematic sampling for in-depth interviews. Sixteen to twenty-five year old people cannot be withdrawn from the club for systematic interviewing in the way that children can be withdrawn from the classroom. It seemed highly unlikely that a representative sample could be constituted by inviting the membership to respond to an appointment system of interviews. The second problem is that it would require an inordinate length of time with each individual to cover by the interview method the wide range of areas identified in the previous section. The third problem is that, even if it were possible to interview a representative sample of the members over the whole range of issues, the length of time taken by such interviews would result in the total sample studied being quite small.

The in-depth interview is an important second stage, after the participant observation stage, as a way of sharpening the issues with which the project should be concerned. I conducted a series of in-depth interviews in order to become more alert to the questions I ought to be asking the young people and the kind of answers that they are likely to give. But, again, I decided that this should not be the level on which I would ultimately rest the research I was to undertake. Therefore, I turned my attention to the third research technique.

The third method is that of the questionnaire, which young people could fill in themselves during their own time. In particular I grew to favour the kind of questionnaire which uses mainly closed, rather than open ended questions. By this, I mean the kind of questionnaire which does not expect the person filling it in to write their own answers, but rather to select from a range of given replies. This sort of questionnaire is difficult to draw up, but once carefully prepared, it is very easy to use.

The main advantages of this kind of questionnaire are these. It is possible to collect detailed information from a much larger sample of young people. The fact that the answers are pre-coded means that it is a relatively easy task to deal with a large number of replies and that nothing is left to the arbitrary interpretation of those preparing the data for analysis. In the design of the closed form of questionnaire, it is possible to ask a number of questions over a wide range of topics, defining each question in a precise and unambiguous way. Careful design of the questionnaire makes it possible to build into it objective methods of testing for carelessness, untruthfulness, inconsistencies, and so on. The fact that the self-completion questionnaire can be filled in at any time enables the young person to respond to the questions when and where they really have the time to do so. Finally, once a questionnaire has been carefully constructed, it is possible to repeat the study easily. For example, it would now be possible to repeat the study in the Centymca Club in a specific number of years time to chart the way in which attitudes may be changing. Similarly, it would be possible to repeat the study in other places to examine the differences and similarities with the London situation.

The questionnaire employed in the project evolved slowly and through a whole series of discussions and pilot testings. On the basis of the insights which I gained from the time I spent in the Centymca Club as a participant observer and as clinical interviewer, I drew up draft forms of a questionnaire. These drafts were discussed with people concerned with the voluntary and statutory youth service, unemployment among young people, or survey work in educational research. Pilot applications of the questionnaire were tried first in schools and among college classes. Finally, the questionnaire was tested out among members of the Centymca Club itself.

Many changes were made during the development of the questionnaire before the final version evolved, known as the 'Centymca Attitude Inventory'. In the Centymca Attitude Inventory, the twelve key areas discussed in the previous chapter were each studied by means of a battery of carefully chosen questions. These questions were randomised so that the items relating to the distinct areas did not cluster together, and so they did not become immediately obvious to the young people completing the questionnaire. The Centymca Attitude Inventory also contained a section designed to collect detailed background information about the young people, including details about their employment and about their history of unemployment.

After the questionnaire had been carefully designed, the research programme itself was ready to begin. The method of distributing the questionnaire to the Centymca Club members was to give them personally a copy when they either joined the Club for the first time or renewed their membership. Each questionnaire was numbered, and a record card was kept of the name and address of the person to whom each questionnaire was given. The number was used to know who had not returned the questionnaire, so that reminder letters could be mailed to them. The young people were assured that, once their questionnaire had been returned, the number would be detached to preserve complete anonymity.

Completion of the Centymca Attitude Inventory was in no way compulsory. In fact the questionnaire was not given out with the membership application forms, but at the time when the person had already been accepted into membership, paid a membership fee and received a membership certificate. 40.4% of the sample returned their completed questionnaires without reminding. A reminder letter, sent after a month, resulted in a further 7.9%. Finally, six weeks or so after the first reminder letter, a second copy of the questionnaire was posted to those who had still not replied, together with a stamped addressed reply envelope. The second reminder letter drew completed questionnaires from a further 9% of the members.

Thus, all told, there was a response rate of 57.3%. In terms of the average response rate to questionnaires completed in the respondent's own time, and regarding which there is no compulsion to reply, this represents an exceptionally good return, particularly in view of the length of the questionnaire and the sensitivity of some of the items.

ASKING THE RIGHT PEOPLE

Over the period of time that was available for data collection, the response rate of 57.3% resulted in there being available for analysis 1,085 completed questionnaires from the young people aged between sixteen and twenty-five years. A close inspection of just who these young people are confirms our contention that London Central YMCA attracts a truly wide clientele and forms an appropriate context for the research project. In this section I propose to provide a brief description of those who completed the questionnaire.

From being an all male organisation in the nineteenth century, the London Central YMCA has grown steadily into an association which caters equally for men and for women. In the sixteen to twenty-five year age group, the balance between the sexes has been almost perfectly achieved, although the odds are still slightly weighted in favour of the men. For every eleven male members there are nine female members in this age group.

Just as the YMCA has ceased being an all male organisation, so it is no longer an all Christian organisation. In response to the direct question 'Are you a practising member of a religious group?' two-thirds of the young people firmly answered that they were not. Out of the 1,085 young members, 294 claimed allegiance to the Christian faith. The two largest Christian groups were made up of 132 members of the Church of England and 118 members of the Roman Catholic Church. The other Christian denominations were represented by only a few members each. A further eighty-eight of them claimed allegiance to one of the other world religions. The two largest non-Christian groups were made up of thirty-seven Moslems and thirty Jews. There were also seven Buddhist, five Hindu and five Sikh members.

Not only do the young members represent a wide variety of religious backgrounds, they also represent a wide variety of national backgrounds. Just over a third of the young members had been born outside England, Scotland, Wales or Northern Ireland. These 380 foreign born young people described themselves as coming from sixty-three countries across the world. The three countries most strongly represented were Malaysia, Iran and Hong Kong. The next most frequently named countries were Cyprus, Eire, Germany, India, Indonesia, Italy, Nigeria and the United States of America. Just over a third of the young people who had been born overseas had now been living in Great Britain for more than five years. Nearly two-thirds of them, therefore, were still relative newcomers to this country.

Although the study is based on young people living in London in the early 1980s, it is in no sense restricted to 'Londoners'. Less than one-third of the young members had lived in London all their lives. In fact, 57% had lived in London for less than five years, while 16% had lived in London for less than one year. The young people who had not lived in London all their lives had moved there from a number of different backgrounds, ranging from other large cities to small villages. The sample, therefore, represents a wide spectrum of experience and expectations about living in different sorts of communities. The 420 young people who had moved to London from another part of England had come from all over the country.

When the young people go home from the Centymca Club, they go back to a number of different home environments. Three hundred and twenty-four of them were still living at home with their parents. Four hundred and seventy-six had moved away from their parent's home to establish somewhere of their own, which the married young people were sharing with their own family and the single ones were sharing with other people of their own age. A further ninety-two lived in houses or flats alone, while fifty-six were living alone in bedsitters. One hundred and thirty were living in some form of hostel or hall of residence.

More than three-quarters of the young people lived within a ten mile radius of the centre of London (Oxford Circus).

Another indication of the wide range of young people who come into membership of the Centymca Club is given by an analysis of their occupations. To begin with, there was a very interesting mix between students and young workers. Three in every ten of the respondents were students, while the other seven were either in employment or seeking employment. A number of the young people who came to central London did so to further their education, either as full-time or part-time students. The educational range of the membership is, therefore, extraordinarily wide. At one end of the spectrum, 162 of the young people held first degrees, while a further twenty-four actually held a higher degree. At the other end of the educational spectrum, 149 of the young members had not been educated up to O level standard. This wide range of educational ability was also clearly reflected in the kinds of work the young people are doing; the sample included a most remarkable range of people working in many different jobs.

To sum up, the sample includes men and women from a great range of national, credal, educational and social backgrounds. There are students as well as young workers in the sample. A wide variety of different occupations are represented, from the least skilled manual jobs to the most highly skilled and professional vocational pursuits. As well as single young people, the sample includes some who are married, living together or divorced. At the same time it includes young people living in a number of different environments and types of accommodation.

The key question which now needs to be asked, of course, is to what extent this group contains young people who have recent experience of unemployment. The answer to this question is that almost one-third (31.5%) of the 1,085 young people who completed the Centymca Attitude Inventory had in fact experienced periods of unemployment during the past two years. For the majority of them, this experience of unemployment had been between one and six months in duration. However, 10.2% of the respondents had been unemployed for more than six months of the previous two years, and some of these young people had been unemployed for the whole of that period. Expressed in another way, 21.3% of the total sample had recent experience of short-term unemployment, while 10.2% of them had recent experience of long-term unemployment. Having discovered this important piece of information, it is now the task of the next chapter to study in-depth who these unemployed young people actually are, and how they relate to the rest of the sample.

3. The Young Unemployed

The previous chapter ended by providing a careful description of the total sample of young people who co-operated in the present study and by revealing that almost one in three of them reported recent experience of unemployment. The intention of the present chapter is to examine in detail the group who have been recently unemployed: do the young unemployed stand out as a group different from those who have not shared this experience?

The answer is both yes and no. The answer is yes, in as much as there are indeed certain groups of young people among whom the incidence of unemployment is higher. The answer is no, in as much as there appear to be no groups of young people who seem to be guaranteed immunity from unemployment in the present economic and social climate. Indeed, a really significant point to emerge from the analysis of the present data is that, in the 1980s, unemployment is most certainly no respecter of persons among sixteen to twenty-five year old young people. No particular categories or groups of young people are totally immune from experiencing periods of being out of work.

In this sample of 1,085 young people, unemployment had affected the lives of men and women, sixteen and twenty-five year olds. It had affected the married as well as the single; those who were living together and those who were separated or divorced. It had affected the lives of those who left school at sixteen without any academic qualifications at all, and those who left university at twenty-two with a good honours degree. It had affected the lives of those who were born in England, as well as those who were born overseas and were newcomers to London. It had affected the lives of those who lived at home with their parents and those who lived alone; those who lived in bedsitters and those who shared flats or houses with others. It had affected the lives of those who were working in the most prestigious and well-paid posts, as well as those in the most menial and poorly paid employment.

The very fact that as many as 31.5% of the total membership of the Centymca Club have had recent experience of unemployment serves to emphasize the extremely widespread nature of unemployment among sixteen to twenty-five year olds at the centre of London. However, while accepting the importance of the point that unemployment reaches the most diverse kinds of young people, it is still of great importance to draw attention to the characteristics of those young people who are the most vulnerable to unemployment.

BACKGROUND CHARACTERISTICS

The intention of this section is to review the relationship between the experience of unemployment and the major sociological features which enable us to predict who has and who has not experienced unemployment in the Centymca membership. It is important to remember that what we are looking at in this section is not the question 'Who is unemployed now?' but 'Who has been unemployed at some stage within the last two years?' The ten features which emerge as being of importance are: sex, age, marital status, home background, nationality, familiarity with London, education, socio-economic status, income and accommodation.

A helpful notion to enable us to grasp the significance of the statistics presented in this chapter is the concept of 'prediction'. What we are trying to do is to recognise which of the 1,085 young people on whom we have detailed information were most likely to be part of the 31.5% who had a recent history of being unemployed. If we had no clues at all on which to work, and we pointed at the young people around us in a random fashion, we would expect to be right about once every three times, since we know that about one in every three of the total membership has had this unemployment experience. However, by absorbing carefully what we can learn from the following sections about the relationship between such factors as sex, marital status, home background and so on, we can improve our chances of pointing out the right young people from the crowd and, thus, increase our power of prediction.

Sex

To begin with, the women members of the Centymca club are much more likely to have experienced periods of unemployment during the past two years than the men. 37% of the women reported that they had been unemployed during this period, compared with 27% of the men.

Age

Age is another important factor to have in mind when trying to predict the likelihood of one of the 1,085 young people having been recently unemployed. The young people at the lower end of the ten year age band under review are more vulnerable to unemployment than the young people at the higher end of this ten year period. In this way, 37% of the eighteen to nineteen year olds reported that they had been unemployed during the past two years, compared with 32% of the twenty-two and twenty-three year olds and 25% of the twenty-four and twenty-five year olds.

Marital status

Unemployment seems to affect equally the young members of the Centymca club who are married and those who are single. About 30% of the single and 29% of the married young people had recent experience of unemployment. Where there is a significant difference in the level of unemployment is among the young people who said that they are living together without being married. 38% of those who were living together reported that they had been unemployed at some stage during the past two years.

Home background

There is a slightly higher incidence of unemployment among those young people who came from broken homes. 35% of the young people who reported that their parents were divorced or separated had experienced periods of unemployment during the past two years, compared with 31%

of those who reported that their parents are not separated or divorced.

Nationality

The young members of the Centymca club who were born in Great Britain fare considerably better in the employment stakes than those who were born overseas. This difference becomes most apparent when we compare the proportions of the British born young people and the foreign born young people who had experienced long-term unemployment during the past two years. 8.2% of the British born young people have experienced long-term unemployment, compared with 13.4% of those born overseas. The length of their period of residence in Britain is also related to the ease with which the foreign born young people can find employment. It is the newcomers to Britain who found the greatest difficulty in finding work, with 17.3% of those who have been resident in England for less than three years having experienced long-term unemployment.

Familiarity with London

London is still a city which attracts young people who come seeking work, but who have very little prospect of finding it. The young people who have grown up in London, or who have made it their home for some time, are much less likely to be seeking work unsuccessfully than the newcomers to the city.

The time that it seems to take to become established in London is about three years. Only 27% of the young people who had lived in London for more than three years reported a recent experience of unemployment, compared with 33% of those who had lived in London for more than two years but less than three. The really vulnerable groups of young people are those who are relative newcomers to the city. As many as 42% of those who had lived in London for less than two years reported recent experiences of unemployment, while 57% of those who had just arrived in the city have a recent history of unemployment.

Education

Educational achievement is by no means a straightforward predictor of the young person's vulnerability to unemployment. What seems to be the case is a curvilinear relationship. This means that the young people who were most likely to have experienced unemployment within the past two years were those at either end of the spectrum of educational qualifications. 35% of the young people who left school without having reached O level standard had recent experience of unemployment, and so had 35% of those who had stayed on at university to obtain higher degrees.

The young people who had obtained a few O levels are hardly any better off than those who had obtained none. The real difference comes between those who had a few O levels and those who had five or more O level passes. While 34% of the young people with only a few O levels had recent experience of unemployment, only 26% of those with five or more O levels were in this situation. In fact it seems that the young people who had obtained five or more O levels, but who then had stopped improving their academic qualifications were in the best position regarding employability. Those who had stayed on in education to obtain A levels were considerably more likely to have experienced unemployment then those who withdrew from education after their O level successes. 31% of the young people with A levels had recent experience of unemployment, and the situation of graduates was slightly worse, with 32% of the first degree holders having this experience.

Socio-economic status

Socio-economic status is often determined in social research on the basis of the social grading of different forms of employment. There are several occupational classification systems in current use, but the most frequently used scale is the five point categorisation proposed by the Government Office of Population, Censuses and Surveys. It is this system which is currently used in the analysis of many official statistics. This scale is a classification of occupations (or to be more precise of 'unit groups' of occupations) according to 'the general standing within the community of the occupations concerned'.

According to this classification system, professionals like doctors, accountants, solicitors and clergymen, are assigned to social class one. Semi-professionals, like teachers, social workers, journalists and entertainers, are assigned to social class two. Social class three includes bus drivers, clerks, secretaries and electricians. Social class four includes postmen, machine operators, bricklayers and bus conductors. Social class five includes unskilled manual labourers, porters and messengers.

Since the Centymca Attitude Inventory made available detailed information about the young members' jobs it was possible to assign each of those who was currently employed to a socio-economic category.

Although the young person's educational attainment is not a straightforward predictor of their vulnerability towards the experience of unemployment, the socio-economic status of their present work is a much stronger predictor. The young people who had successfully moved into the higher social class occupations were more permanently secure in their work than those in the lower social class jobs. In this way, only 18% of the young people working in social class one occupations had experienced any period of unemployment during the past two years, compared with 35% of those in social class two or three occupations and 43% of those working in social class four or five occupations.

Income

Just as the socio-economic status of the young person's current occupation proved to be a useful indicator of their vulnerability to the experience of unemployment, so does knowledge of their current level of income help to distinguish between those who were likely to have been recently unemployed and those who were not. The young people with a current take-home pay packet which placed them within the bottom fifth of the income range of the Centymca members were most vulnerable to being unemployed, while those in the top fifth of the income range were least likely to have been unemployed. 31% of the young people in the middle three-fifths of the income range had experienced unemployment during the past two years, compared with 36% of those in the bottom fifth of the income range and 23% of those in the top fifth of the income range.

Accommodation

Another interesting factor, which seems to help us to predict the young people who were more likely to have experienced unemployment during the past two years, was knowledge of the kind of accommodation in which they lived. Those least likely to have experienced unemployment were the young people who lived with their parents, with their own family or in a house or flat alone. 29% of the young people who lived with their parents, 29% of the young people who lived alone and 30% of the young people who lived with their own family reported that they had been unemployed at some time during the past two years.

The young people who lived in shared accommodation, hostels or bedsitters were much more likely to have experienced unemployment. Thus, 34% of those who shared a house or flat with other young people who are not part of their own family, had experienced some unemployment during the past two years. Similarly, 35% of those who lived in hostels and 36% of those who lived in bedsitters had been unemployed during this period.

CUMULATIVE PICTURE

The cumulative picture which emerges from keeping the ten factors reviewed above in mind begins to become quite impressive. We can now begin to piece together the identikit features of the young people most vulnerable to unemployment.

The most vulnerable of the Centymca members to unemployment are the sixteen to nineteen year old women who were born overseas and were relative newcomers to England, who left school at sixteen without any academic qualifications, whose parents are divorced, who had recently come to London without real prospects of work, who were living with their boyfriend in a bedsitter, and who were currently working in a low status and poorly paid job.

The fact that this kind of stereotype has emerged is both interesting and impressive. However, it must be realised that stereotypes can both distort reality as well as help us to understand reality. Not every young person who fits that stereotype has necessarily had recent experience of unemployment. Moreover, not every young person who is the very antithesis to that stereotype is necessarily immune from the experience of unemployment. All that the stereotype has done is to make us more alert to the characteristics of vulnerability.

The other important fact to keep in mind is that the ten points which have helped us to distinguish between those at high risk and those at low risk of unemployment are by no means unrelated among themselves. We have reviewed one feature at a time purely for the purposes of analytic convenience. What we must do now is to find a more sophisticated technique to enable us to recognise whether any of these features are redundant, and to give us some measure of how adequately those ten features actually improve our ability to identify the young people most at risk. The appropriate statistical technique for this job is known as 'discriminant analysis'.

The mathematical objective of discriminant analysis is to weight and linearly combine the discriminating variables in some fashion so that the groups are forced to be as statistically distinct as possible. Discriminant analysis is able to tell us three important additional things about the ten issues listed above and about their combined power to 'discriminate' between the young people who have experienced unemployment and those who have not. First, when used in a stepwise fashion, this statistical technique helps us to identify which of the ten issues are the most useful in predicting the young people who are most likely to have experienced unemployment. Second, the technique helps us to see the most economical and useful combination which can be formed from the ten variables to pick out most accurately the young people who have been unemployed.

The third useful additional piece of information which discriminant analysis makes available to us is a measure of the overall usefulness of the variables which we are using to predict unemployment. It does this by picking out the young people from the data file to whom the most appropriate combination of the ten variables would point as being the most vulnerable to unemployment. It is then a simple matter to compare the predictions made by the technique with our information about whether or not the young people picked out had in fact recent experience of unemployment. This is a very practical way of testing out the value of the ten factors identified in this chapter for actually predicting the vulnerability to unemployment among young people.

Having grasped the idea of what this statistical technique is able to do, we must examine the information which it makes available to us. First of all, it places the ten disriminating variables in their order of usefulness. This tells us that knowledge of the social class classification of the young person's present employment is the most useful piece of information in predicting their vulnerability to unemployment, and in second place to this is information about their current rate of take home pay. Close behind these two factors come information about their age and sex, and then information about their home background and where they currently live.

According to this combination of factors, we would look first for young people in low social class jobs who are earning a low level of income. From this group we would then look for the younger women who come from broken homes and who are living in bedsitters.

The second piece of information given to us by discriminant analysis is that, once we know the six things about young people listed in the previous paragraph, knowledge about the other four factors, namely their nationality, their academic qualifications, their marital status and the time they have lived in London, does not improve any further our ability to pick out the unemployed. This is not to say that these four factors have ceased to be significant in their own right. Indeed, these factors may well in their turn have helped to lead the young person into low prestige and low income work. What it does say, however, it that once we know what sort of work they are doing and how much they are earning, extra information about their nationality, qualifications, marital status and length of residence in London is redundant. In other words, it is more information than we actually need.

The third piece of information to be given to us by discriminant analysis is very important indeed, since it warns us against putting too much faith in the stereotype of the young unemployed which comes from concentrating on the picture drawn from these ten discriminating factors. The point is that knowledge of the ten factors improves our ability to pick out the unemployed young people from the group around us, but it only improves our prediction by a very small amount. When we have all ten pieces of information about the young members of the Centymca club and use this information as the basis on which to predict who is most likely to have had recent experience of unemployment, we are not going to be correct in our predictions many more times than if we just pointed to young people at random. In this way, discriminant analysis provides further confirmation of the point that in the 1980s unemployment among young people is no respecter of persons.

PSYCHOLOGICAL CHARACTERISTICS

DOES IT?

The next six chapters turn attention from an examination of the sociological characteristics of the young unemployed to an examination of their psychological characteristics. Each of these six chapters reviews one of the specific sets of psychological characteristics which the Centymca Attitude Inventory was designed to assess. To some extent, the order in which these six sets of issues are reviewed is quite arbitrary. The reader may well decide to plan his or her route through these chapters in whatever order the issues most appeal.

In order to test the relationship between attitudes and the experience of unemployment, the total sample of 1,085 young people was divided into three groups rather than just two groups. The point is that it began to become clear from the data that we were in fact dealing with two different types of experience of unemployment among young people. There are those whose experience of unemployment may be called 'short-term' and those whose experience is more long-term. In some situations the attitudes of those who have experienced short-term and long-term unemployment differ as much from each other as the difference between those who have not experienced unemployment at all and those who have. The data also seem to suggest that the most helpful cut-off point in distinguishing between those who had short-term experience of unemployment and those who had long-term experience is somewhere about half a year.

The comparisons described in the following chapters are, therefore, based on the three following groups: 68.5% of the sample which had experienced no unemployment during the previous two years; 21.3% of the sample who had experienced short-term unemployment covering up to six months of the previous two years; 10.2% of the sample who had experienced long-term unemployment covering between six and twenty-four months of the previous two years.

When making comparisons between the responses of these three groups, the usual statistical tests of significance have been used, namely t-test and chi square significance tests as appropriate within different situations. Real differences have only been reported as existing between the groups if the 5% probability level has been reached. In cases where this level has not been reached, it has been assumed that differences between the groups are not likely to be the result of anything other than chance fluctuations. This means that confidence can be placed in the differences reported.

4. Well-being and Worry

WELL-BEING

Well-being is a concept which is being increasingly employed in psychological research. It is used to sum up the individual's basic attitude to life. As a way of talking about the general level of satisfaction which people derive from their lives, this is a particularly important area for scrutiny in our examination of the psychological correlates of the experience of unemployment. For example, the relationship between being out of work and the reporting of lower levels of well-being has already been explored by Peter Warr's study of redundant steelworkers. The results of this study are reported in an important paper in the British Journal of Psychology for 1978, under the title 'A Study of Psychological Well-being'.

One of the points which Peter Warr makes when introducing his study is concerned with what he calls 'the somewhat malleable' notion of the concept of well-being itself. Like so much of the jargon employed in psychological research, the term well-being is used by different writers with different meanings. Especially since my own use is different from Peter Warr's, I need to be careful to specify the way in which I am employing the concept.

Some researchers use the concept of well-being to bring together a wide range of psychological components which are to do with people's feelings about their every day life and activities. This use would include specifics like worries, job satisfaction, personal esteem and the enjoyment of leisure time. In some situations such a broad definition can be very useful, but my own preference is to deal with issues like leisure, work, worry and self image separately. My reason for making this choice is not a denial of the importance of these other components in formulating a total impression of well-being, but rather the belief that a clearer picture emerges if we can deal with only a small part of the total picture at at time.

The kind of questions I decided to ask under this heading of well-being were, therefore, general questions concerned with the young person's overall response to life. I started my examination of well-being with the very general question 'I find life really worth living'. It needs to be remembered at this point that the young people were given the opportunity of responding to questions on the five point scale of 'agree strongly', 'agree', 'not certain', 'disagree' and 'disagree strongly'. The responses to this first question are very illuminating. There is a clear association between the young persons' response to this question and the length of their experience of unemployment. As their period of unemployment increases, so their likelihood of agreeing that they find life really worth living decreases. While 38% of those who have no experience of unemployment agree strongly that they find life really worth living, this is the case for only 34% of those who have experienced short-term unemployment, and 31% of those who have experienced long-term unemployment.

One of the major reasons why the unemployed have a generally lower sense of satisfaction from living is that being out of work erodes their sense of purpose. In our present society, work is a very important factor in giving structure, shape and meaning to life. The young people who lack work are also significantly more likely to say that they lack a sense of purpose in life.

After leaving school, for many people it is work that provides an important reference for their social life. It is through their work that they meet people, make friends and escape from isolation and loneliness. For this reason, I was interested in the replies to the question 'I tend to be a lonely person'. Again a clear trend emerged in the expected direction. The longer the young people were unemployed, the lonelier they tended to become. While only 3% of those who had no experience of unemployment claimed to be acutely lonely, this proportion rose to 6% of those who had experienced short-term unemployment and 8% of those who had experienced long-term unemployment.

Together with the erosion of their sense of purpose in life and the accentuation of their feelings of loneliness, the unemployed young people are more likely to feel that their

whole personal worth and identity is being undermined.
The young people's replies to the question 'I feel I am not
worth much as a person' reveal two interesting facts. The
experience of short-term unemployment begins to shake
their self confidence; the short-term unemployed are more
likely than those who have not experienced unemployment to
check the uncertain response to this question. While they
are less likely than those who have no recent experience of
unemployment to positively assert their worth as a person,
the short-term unemployed are not more likely to dismiss
themselves as worthless. On the other hand, it is the
long-term unemployed who are found to be much more
thoroughly critical of themselves. Thus, while only 6% of
the short-term unemployed and 6% of the employed say that
they feel they are not worth much as a person, 12% of the
long-term unemployed feel this way about themselves.

One of the key concepts used in the literature to discuss
the psychological correlates of unemployment is that of
depression. A problem in interpreting some research has
been to obtain a measure of the extent to which young
people say that they feel depressed anyway and against
which the reported depression of the young unemployed can
be assessed. According to the present study a high
proportion of sixteen to twenty-five year olds say that
periods of depression affect them. Thus, 24% of the young
people who have had no recent experience of unemployment
report that they often feel depressed. What is more
significant, however, is that a substantially higher
proportion of those who have experienced unemployment feel
this way about their lives. Depression is an immediate
response to unemployment. 34% of the short-term
unemployed and 34% of the long-term unemployed suffer in
this way.

An accurate indication of the reality and depth of
depression experienced by people is the frequency with
which they are troubled by suicidal thoughts. Just as the
unemployed are more likely than the employed to report
frequent periods of depression, so they are more likely to
report suicidal tendencies. Already 17% of the young
people who have had no recent experience of unemployment
admit that they sometimes feel so bad about life and so
depressed that they have sometimes considered taking their
own lives. However, the proportion is again sharply

increased among the young unemployed. 24% of the
short-term unemployed and 26% of the long-term unemployed
have sometimes considered taking their own lives.

The relationship between unemployment and suicide is an
issue which is thoroughly debated in the literature. On the
one hand, a number of studies indicate that unemployment
is related not only to the incidence of suicidal thoughts,
but also to attempted suicides and fatal suicides. For
example, Sainsbury's study of suicide in London, published
in 1955, found that the unemployed has a much higher
suicide rate than the employed and that in about one-third
of the unemployed suicides, unemployment was given as the
principal cause. Sainsbury further supports his thesis by
an analysis of the Registrar General's annual statistics
which show a rise in suicide during the depression of
1930-32. More recently Sathyvathi's study in 1977 of the
relationship between unemployment and suicide in Bangalore
adds further evidence for this relationship.

On the other hand, there are some reports which do not
support the notion of an increased suicide rate during
periods of unemployment. An important study in this
category is that of Walbran, MacMahon and Bailey who
found no correlation between suicide rates and
unemployment in Pennsylvania between 1954 and 1961. At
the same time, Hayes and Nutman's review of the
psychological effects of unemployment points to the possible
circularity in the situation. They would argue, rightly,
that a correlational study like my own only demonstrates
which phenomena go together; it does no prove causality.
They write that 'the nature of the relationship is difficult to
define. Is the high incidence of unemployed persons
committing suicide due to their unemployed status, or do
factors that lead to suicide also make it difficult for them to
sustain employment, or is it an interdependence of the
two?' This is clearly an issue which still desperately
warrants further intensive examination.

WORRY

There is a sense in which a high level of worry can be
seen as one of the important indicators of a low level of
general well-being. On the other hand, it is worthwhile to

separate out the idea of worry and to review it in its own right, since worry is often seen as specifically directed towards certain objects or areas. This section, therefore, reviews not only how much the sixteen to twenty-five year olds worry but also what they worry about. To what extent is the content and level of their worries related to the difficulty they have experienced in finding work?

The most obvious source of anxiety associated with the experience of unemployment is to do with the financial constraints imposed by the loss or absence of an earned income. As the length of unemployment increases, so it becomes increasingly difficult to maintain any standard of living without running the risk of building up debts and overdrafts, especially at the heart of the expensive city life. There is quite a tendency anyway for young people during the years immediately after leaving school to be unable to manage their financial affairs wisely, and consequently to begin to build up debts. The experience of unemployment exacerbates the problem. 21% of the young people who had no recent experience of unemployment complained that they were worried about the debts they had already incurred. This proportion rises slightly to 23% of the short-term unemployed and more sharply to include 29% of the long-term unemployed. In dealing with the unemployed young people we need to be aware of the extent to which financial hardship impinges upon their lives.

The way in which unemployment affects the young person's relationships with other people is also a significant cause for additional worry. Not only does job loss cut the young person off from a significant source of making friends and of maintaining friendships, it also curtails significant aspects of their social lives by imposing financial restraints. Just as the young person needs his or her friends more, so the loss of income restricts the social activities in which they can afford to engage and by which they are able to interact with their friends. With this goes an accentuated anxiety about relationships in general. The unemployed young people were more inclined to report that they were worried about their relationships with other people than those who have not been out of work. Moreover, alongside the pressures which unemployment places on relationships in general is the special pressure placed on the young person's sex life. 19% of the unemployed young people complain that they are worried about their sex lives compared with 14% of those who have not been unemployed.

A growing body of research has begun to point to the health consequences of unemployment. For example, Stanislav Kasl and Sidney Cobb have contributed considerably to the literature in their series of papers on this issue. They have taken into account the relationship between unemployment and physiological measures like blood pressure and urine samples, social psychological data like the ability to relax with people, and health data like the questionnaire measurement of how well the person feels. There have also been two recent important studies: 'Unemployment and Health' prepared by Malcolm Colledge for the North Tyneside Community Health Council, and 'Unemployment and Health in Families' prepared by Leonard Fagin and Martin Little for the Department of Health and Social Security. Both studies were published in 1981.

One of the conclusions drawn from Leonard Fagin's study is worth reporting in full: 'We were surprised to see how often matters of health became important issues in the families we interviewed, so much so that at times it completely took over the specific reaction to unemployment. It was as if health problems were unwittingly selected as the main avenue of expression of the obvious distress that most of these families were experiencing. We thought that this deserved special attention as the implications of these findings on the Health Services and the families themselves were far-reaching and severe.'

Against this background, it seemed a matter of vital significance to include in our survey indices of the extent to which the young unemployed were expressing worry about their physical or mental health, and the extent to which they differed in their level of anxiety from their employed contemporaries. All the indications in the survey are in the expected direction. To begin with, a higher proportion of the unemployed young people claim that they are worried about their health in a general sense. This is the case for 29% of the long-term unemployed, compared with 24% of those who have no recent experience of unemployment.

The unemployed young people are also much more worried about their ability to cope with life and about the risk they run of facing a nervous breakdown. 17% of the long-term unemployed and 15% of the short-term unemployed say that they are worried that they cannot cope, compared with 11% of those who have not had recent experience of unemployment. 16% of the long-term unemployed and 12% of the short-term unemployed are worried that they might have a breakdown, compared with 8% of those who have no recent experience of unemployment. In terms of the health consequences of unemployment, the long-term unemployed young people consider themselves to be much closer to a breakdown than their employed contemporaries. Looked at another way, the long-term unemployed young people are twice as likely as the employed young people to be worrying about their mental health. It is precisely this kind of anxiety which is likely to push them further along the road to an inability to cope with life and to be in need of external psychological support and help.

Two further questions were included in the review of worry in order to explore more precisely the way in which health anxieties are given expression by the young unemployed. The first question explored their level of anxiety about the risks of getting cancer. In fact 34% of the short-term unemployed and 32% of the long-term unemployed said that they were worred about this issue. However, this is also the case for 33% of the young people who have not experienced unemployment. The fear of cancer is very much uppermost in the minds of young people as a health risk, but their level of anxiety about this risk is in no way related to their employment history.

The second question examined the extent to which the young people are worried about growing old. Their replies to this question clearly indicate that anxiety about old age is related to the difficulty they have experienced in finding work. 26% of the young people who had not experienced recent difficulty in finding work reported that they were worried about growing old. This proportion increases to 29% among the short-term unemployed and to 34% among the long-term unemployed.

So far this review has indicated that the young unemployed tend to be greater worriers than their employed contemporaries in terms of their anxiety about their financial matters, their relationships and their health. All of these are very personal areas of worry. To what extent does the experience of unemployment drive young people to worry more about things outside themselves as well, or do they tend to become so absorbed with inward looking anxieties that they tend to attribute less significance to potential sources of anxiety outside themselves?

As a way of testing this issue, the young people were asked to assess the extent to which they actually worried about the general situation of the world in which they live. Their replies to this question are very revealing. The unemployed young people are less inclined to worry about things outside themselves. 66% of those who had not been unemployed reported that they were worried about the world situation, compared with 61% of those who had recent experience of unemployment. Increased anxiety about one's own ability to survive goes hand in hand with a decreased anxiety about world survival and world problems. While the young unemployed are taking their own problems more seriously, at the same time they are taking world problems less seriously.

5. Self Image and Counselling

SELF IMAGE

Just like well-being, self image is a term which has come to have a wide range of meanings in the work of different psychologists. Once again, I must be careful to specify how I am going to use the term and how my use differs from the concept as employed by other researchers.

To begin with, there are two related terms from which I need to distinguish my use of the term self image. These are self esteem and self concept. The problem is that both of these other terms have been recently used in the study of the psychological consequences of unemployment by other researchers. For example, Jean Hartley in her work on the impact of unemployment on managers speaks about their self esteem; while Kingsley, who is also working with unemployed managers, speaks of their self concept. Self concept is the broader term and self esteem the narrower, but both concentrate on the idea of personal evaluation, the way in which people feel about themselves.

In my usage, self image is not concerned so much with the way young people directly feel about themselves. I am more concerned to gauge the degree to which young people try to project a socially desirable image of themselves to the world at the cost of being truthful about themselves. The young people may be aware of the disparity between what they are saying about themselves and the truth of the matter, or they may not be so self-aware. In either case, by looking at their self image, we are looking directly at the way in which they wish others to perceive them. This use of the term touches on a very wide literature; in particular it draws upon A.L. Edwards' discussion of Social Desirability and H.J. Eysenck's discussion of the Lie Scale in the measurement of personality and social attitudes. For the purposes of the present study, an examination of the young person's self image is important for two reasons.

First, a major problem in attitude research concerns the

way in which people are sometimes afraid to let their real feelings be known in case the researcher should disapprove of them. This problem affects research conducted both by interviews and by questionnaire methods. In this context, the self image questions act as a kind of index of lying and help the researcher to tease out who is telling the truth and who is not.

Second, self image questions help us to assess how secure people feel in themselves. Some people need the support and approval of others much more deeply and urgently. It is these people who more often try to pretend that they are better people than they really are. They try so hard to win the support and approval of others that they cease to tell the truth about themselves. On this understanding, questions to do with self image help us to assess the way in which the experience of unemployment may threaten the confidence which young people have in themselves and the extent to which it may lead to deep feelings of insecurity.

A range of standard questions has been developed in the research literature to gauge this notion of self image. The kind of areas often explored in this context are those characteristics which are usually deemed socially unacceptable, but which at the same time few people can truthfully deny. Precise areas which I decided to include in my own test of self image were telling lies, breaking promises, stealing, feelings of jealousy and resentment and taking advantage of others. The theory is that the more of these characteristics denied by young people, the more under threat those young people seem to be.

Looking at the replies of the 1,085 young people, the overall impression is that they are not trying to project a socially desirable image of themselves at the cost of truthfulness. A few young people made unrealistic claims about themselves, but they represented a very small proportion of the total sample. For example, about 4% of the total group claimed that they had never told a lie. This is the kind of proportion we would expect in the present type of survey work. Perhaps some of these really are people who are scrupulously honest in their dealings with others; perhaps others lack the self insight to be really aware of when they have told lies; perhaps the third group knows that lying is generally disapproved of and they are afraid to run the risk of facing disapproval if they admit to such a characteristic in themselves. The real point, however, is that the low level of people professing such a socially desirable and yet unlikely characteristic gives us no reason to suspect that there has been a wholesale attempt on the part of the young people filling in the questionnaire to distort their replies in order to appear to be better people than they really are.

The second point to emerge from an analysis of the replies. to the six questions in this section is that the responses of those who have experienced short-term unemployment do not differ at all significantly from the replies of those who have no recent experience of unemployment. Roughly the same proportions of those who have experienced short-term unemployment and those who have experienced no recent unemployment admit to sometimes telling lies, to sometimes breaking their promises, and to sometimes taking things that do not belong to them. Roughly the same proportions of the two groups admit to sometimes experiencing feelings of jealousy, to sometimes experiencing feelings of resentment and to sometimes taking advantage of other people.

Two conclusions can be drawn from this. The young people who have experienced short-term unemployment do not feel, in this sense, less secure in themselves than those who have not experienced any recent unemployment. They do not experience greater insecurity to the point that they feel a deeper need for the support and the approval of others. The young people who have experienced short-term unemployment are not more likely to need, or wish, to project a socially desirable image of themselves at the cost of sacrificing truthfulness about themselves. At this level, the replies of the short-term unemployed to the questionnaire can be trusted with as much confidence as the replies of those who have had no recent experience of unemployment.

The third point to emerge from an analysis of the replies to the six questions in this section is that the responses of those who had experienced long-term unemployment differ from the replies of the other young people in relationship to three of the questions, while they do not differ in relationship to the other three. The long-term unemployed are not more likely to claim that they had never broken their promises, that they had never taken things which do not belong to them or that they never feel resentment when they do not get their own way. On the other hand, the long-term unemployed are more likely to deny ever telling lies, ever feeling jealous of others or ever taking advantage of people.

In this way, 11% of the long-term unemployed claimed that they had never told a lie, compared with just 3% of the other young people. Only 55% of the long-term unemployed admitted that they sometimes took advantage of people, compared with 61% of those who have experienced short-term unemployment and 62% of those who have no recent experience of unemployment. Only 70% of the long-term unemployed admitted that they had sometimes been jealous of others, compared with 80% of the other young people.

Once again, two conclusions can be drawn from this analysis about the relationship between self image and the experience of long-term unemployment among young people. The young people who had experienced long-term unemployment do appear, in this sense, to be less secure in themselves than those who have either no experience of unemployment or only short-term experience of unemployment. The deeper sense of personal insecurity, which seems to go with the experience of long-term unemployment, is reflected in a more deeply and urgently expressed need for the support and the approval of others. Thus, some of the long-term unemployed appear to be trying harder to win the approval of others at the cost of sacrificing truthfulness about themselves. Their self image has been so threatened that they were less willing to run the risk of incurring the disapproval of others by being totally open and truthful about themselves, and by openly admitting to displaying characteristics in their lives which they believe to be socially unacceptable to others.

This observation also carries with it the implication that some of the replies of the long-term unemployed to the questionnaire could be trusted less thoroughly than the replies of the other young people. This is an important caveat, but only a partial one in light of the fact that only half of the items in this section detect a difference in the responses of the long-term unemployed from the rest of the young people. In summary, there is some evidence to support the relationship between long-term unemployment and a threatened self image among young people, but not enough to invalidate placing a considerable degree of confidence in their replies to the rest of the Centymca Attitude Inventory.

COUNSELLING

As we have already learnt from the sections on well-being, worry and self image, the experience of unemployment seems to erode the young person's sense of purpose in life, undermine their self confidence and accentuate their feelings of loneliness. As a consequence, the unemployed young people are more likely to look to others for support in one way or another. The experience of unemployment increases their feelings of dependency and need. They are more likely to distrust their own judgement, to distrust their ability to make decisions and to distrust their chances of identifying the right course of action.

The two key areas of support identified in the survey were related to the needs for advice and for acceptance, friendship and affection. The young people experienced these areas of support as two quite distinct types of needs which come into extra prominence at different stages during the experience of unemployment. The need to turn to others for advice is something which continues to increase as the experience of unemployment is prolonged. The short-term unemployed are in fact not much more likely to feel the need to turn to others for advice than those who have no recent experience of unemployment. The long-term unemployed are, however, much more likely than the average young person to need to turn to others for advice.

The more basic need for the sort of support that comes through signs of acceptance, friendship and affection sharply increases with the onset of unemployment, and becomes slightly less pronounced as the young person becomes hardened to being unemployed. It is the initial shock of knowing that one is out of work which threatens the self concept. At this stage, it is important to know that others still accept you and are able to support you. What is needed from other people at this stage is not so much constructive advice as more general signs of caring support.

Next, we will turn to an indication of the extent to which the young unemployed reported the need to turn to others for support. 58% of the short-term unemployed felt the need for affection, and 25% of them felt the need for advice. 55% of the long-term unemployed felt the need for affection, and 30% of them felt the need for advice. These statistics need to be compared with the fact that 46% of the young people who have had no recent experience of unemployment reported that they often longed for someone to turn to for affection, and 23% often longed for someone to turn to for advice.

Given the greater needs of the young unemployed to draw upon the support of others, to whom do they turn to meet these needs and from whom do they in fact draw support? Parents are mentioned as a significant source of help by a number of young people, and mothers are generally seen as being more helpful, understanding and approachable than fathers. Thus, 60% of the young members of the Centymca Club reported that they found it helpful to talk about their problems with their mother, and 36% reported that they found it helpful to talk about their problems with their father. The really significant point, however, is that the proportion of unemployed young people who derive help from their parents is no higher than the proportion of employed young people. The greater need experienced by the unemployed is not matched by more parental support.

Even more important to young people than talking their problems through with their parents is the opportunity of talking things through with their close friends. Thus, 77% of the young members of the Centymca Club said that they found it helpful to talk about their problems with close friends. Now the bitter irony of being unemployed is this. It is often the work environment that provides the context in which friendships are made and through which friendships are maintained. The unemployed young people were more likely than the employed to complain that they felt isolated and cut off from friends. It is not surprising, therefore, that the unemployed young people, especially the long-term unemployed young people, are less likely to report that they derived benefit from discussing their problems with their friends. Unemployment creates for the young person a new set of problems and needs, while at the same time it removes one of the primary sources available to them for airing their problems and meeting their needs.

The final aim of this section is to assess the extent to which the young unemployed have turned, or are willing to turn, to professionals for help and advice. As unemployment has become an increasing problem among young people, so formal and informal counselling facilities have slowly sprung up to try to meet the needs of this group. Some of the problems in this area have recently been brought to the attention of the British Psychological Society by Ian Winfield writing in their monthly Bulletin (September, 1981).

What my own data clearly show is that that young unemployed members of the Centymca Club have drawn more frequently on the services of professional counselling facilities than their contemporaries who have not experienced unemployment. The short-term unemployed are significantly more likely to have received help from professional counsellors than those who have not been unemployed, while the long-term unemployed are significantly more likely to have received help from trained counsellors than the short-term unemployed. The actual percentage of young people who have had contact with professional counselling facilities is still quite small and yet it is clearly related to their employment history. Thus, just 9% of the young people without recent experience of unemployment had for one reason or another found it helpful to talk with a trained counsellor, compared with 14% of the short-term unemployed and 20% of the long-term unemployed.

Before the relatively recent burgeoning of the counselling profession, the clergy were one of the primary groups who provided support and advice in times of need. To what extent are the young unemployed still turning in any sense to the church for help? Overall roughly the same proportion of young people claimed to have received help from the clergy as from trained counsellors, that is to say between 11% and 12% of the total group. While the short-term unemployed were less likely to have turned to the clergy than to trained counsellors, the long-term unemployed were just as likely to have turned to the clergy as to the trained counsellor. In this sense the churches still appear to be one of the major agencies actually dealing with the psychological consequences of unemployment among young people.

Since the actual percentage of the unemployed young people who had been helped either by a trained counsellor or a minister of religion was still quite small, it seemed important to examine the perceptions which the young have of these two helping professions. To what extent would the young be willing to turn to the professional for help if ever they desperately needed it?

Overall the clergy have a much worse image among young people than the trained counsellor. In the total sample, 35% of the young members of the Centymca Club reported that they would never discuss their problems with a minister of religion, compared with 21% who report that they would never discuss their problems with a trained counsellor. It seems that, with the best will in the world, the clergy experience greater difficulty in gaining access to young people than counsellors do. However, it is also important to note that the reluctance which young people have to approach the helping professions is to some extent reduced by the experience of unemployment. The young people who had experienced unemployment, however short this experience may have been, appeared less reluctant to approach the professionals than those who had not had this experience. In this way 16% of the unemployed said that they would never approach a trained counsellor to discuss their problems, compared with 23% of the employed. Similarly, only 32% of the unemployed said that they would never approach a minister of religion, compared with 37% of the employed.

Thus, the unemployed young people have actually benefited more from counselling facilities and, at the same time, they have a lower resistance to drawing upon the resources of such facilities. For many of these unemployed young people, however, it had not been easy to find counselling facilities, even when they needed counselling and had been willing to accept it. The unemployed were much more aware, therefore, than other young people of the need both for more counselling facilities and for the better advertising of and the easier access to the facilities which already exist. To be in need of help and be willing to receive it, but not to be in the position to know where and how to obtain it, is a very frustrating and debilitating experience.

6. Values and Beliefs

VALUES

The word 'values' is another of those concepts, like well-being and self image, which has come to have a wide range of meanings in the writings of different psychologists. In the present study the concept of values implies the idea of worth. In this sense, the study of values is to do with the worth people ascribe to different aspects of life. In other words, I am concerned with exploring what young people consider to be important and I want to be able to compare the degree of importance which they attribute to different areas.

In this section there are three main value areas which are singled out for attention. These are economic values, including making money, spending money and saving money, as well as home ownership; personal values, including such factors as family, friends, home and self; and social values, including religion, morality and politics. Values like these are of fundamental concern because they underlie so much of the young person's reponse to daily life. By including this concept in the present study it becomes possible to test how far these fundamental values are related to the young person's experience of unemployment.

First, we shall turn attention to economic values. The financial hardship which goes hand in hand with unemployment has been the subject of a great deal of analysis and discussion. This is, after all, one of the most obvious social and personal consequences of unemployment. A helpful introduction to the literature on this kind of problem is Sinfield's study of the 'Poor and Out of Work in Shields', which he contributed to Peter Townsend's book on The Concept of Poverty. An aspect of the problem which has not been given much attention concerns the effect which unemployment has on the unemployed person's economic values. Given the fact that unemployment reduces their income, do the unemployed young people find themselves attributing more or less importance to money itself?

The three questions included in the Centymca Attitude Inventory to assess this issue invited the young people to consider the importance which they attribute to making money, saving money and spending money. What emerges from their replies to these three questions is a clear curvilinear relationship between the experience of unemployment and economic values. This is to say that a short period of unemployment is related to a lessening of the importance that money plays in the young person's life. The short-term unemployed ascribed significantly less importance to making money, saving money and spending money than those who had no recent experience of unemployment. The long-term unemployed, however, who had presumably incurred greater financial hardship, reasserted the importance of money in their lives. In particular, it becomes important for the long-term unemployed to have money in their pockets to spend. In fact the long-term unemployed ascribed considerably more importance to spending money than either the short-term unemployed or those who had no recent experience of unemployment.

Having described the relative importance ascribed by the three groups to making money, saving money and spending money, it will be helpful to give a more exact indication of their economic values by quoting the proportions of the young people who ascribed importance to each financial area. Saving money was important to 72% of the long-term unemployed, to 65% of the short-term unemployed and to 74% of those who had no recent experience of unemployment. Making money was important to 70% of the long-term unemployed, to 62% of the short-term unemployed and to 67% of those who had no recent experience of unemployment. Spending money was important to 61% of the long-term unemployed, to 53% of the short-term unemployed and to 55% of those who have no recent experience of unemployment.

Another indication of economic values is given by the proportion of young people who think that it is important to invest in their own future through home ownership. Once again, this question produced a curvilinear relationship, according to which the short-term unemployed attributed significantly less importance to home ownership than those who have not experienced unemployment, and the long-term unemployed adopt a position nearer to that of those who had not experienced recent unemployment. In this case, 76% of those who had not been out of work and 73% of those who had been out of work for a long time said that it is important for them to own their own house, compared with 65% of those who had been out of work for a short space of time.

By way of summary, it seems that those who have been out of work for a short space of time tend to minimise the economic implications of their situation by lessening the importance they attribute to economic matters, while the long-term unemployed are more inclined to face this aspect of their situation.

Second, we turn attention from economic values to personal values. Under the umbrella of personal values I propose to review the importance which the young people attribute to their appearance, their reputation, their home and family, their friends, and to having a good time.

The degrees of value attributed to appearance and reputation are good indicators of the way in which the young people see themselves in relationship to others. A number of researchers working in the area of the psychology of unemployment talk in terms of an erosion of self worth. This is the case, for example, in Harrison's study of the demoralising experience of prolonged unemployment, in which he actually speaks in terms of a loss of self worth. Similarly, Bakke's classic study of the unemployed man speaks in terms of loss of self respect, while Eisenberg and Lazarsfeld speak about feelings of inferiority, and Jahoda, Lazarsfeld and Zeisel talk about a loss of morale. If the experience of unemployment is indeed associated with an erosion of self worth, we would expect the unemployed young people to take less trouble over their appearance and to be less concerned about their reputation.

These two predictions were confirmed by the replies to the Centymca Attitude Inventory. As a group, the young members of the Centymca Club generally attributed a great deal of importance to their appearance. In fact, only 3% of those who had no recent experience of unemployment reported that their appearance was not important to them. However, 7% of the short-term unemployed and 6% of the long-term unemployed felt this way about themselves.

Similarly, as a group, the young members of the Centymca Club generally attributed a great deal of importance to their reputation. In fact, 73% of those who had no recent experience of unemployment reported that what people think of them is important to them. However, this proportion falls to 70% of the short-term unemployed and 65% of the long-term unemployed. On both measures, therefore, there is a clear indication that an erosion of self worth was associated with the experience of unemployment.

An erosion of self worth may well be accompanied by a heightened quest for pleasure, excitement and stimulation. A question included in the study to test this possibility read, 'Having a good time is more important than anything else'. The replies to this question indicate that, while the short-term unemployed do not adopt this attitude more frequently than those who had not been unemployed, the long-term unemployed most certainly do. 40% of the long-term unemployed argued that having a good time was more important than anything else, compared with 30% of the short-term unemployed and 33% of those who had not been unemployed.

Studies like those produced by Marsden and Duff and by Fagin and Little argue that the social and psychological consequences of unemployment go beyond the unemployed individual to their family. What effect, then, does being unemployed have on the value that young people ascribe either to their home and family or to their friends? The replies to the Centymca Attitude Inventory suggest very little difference in either case. A very high proportion of the sixteen to twenty-five year olds in the sample reported that they valued both their home and family and their friends a great deal. Moreover, this proportion is neither significantly reduced nor significantly increased by the experience of unemployment. Thus, 91% of the young people who had no recent experience of unemployment reported that their home and family are important to them, and so did 89% of those who had experience of unemployment. 96% of the young people who had no recent experience of unemployment reported that their friends are important to them, and so did 95% of those who had experience of unemployment.

Finally, this section turns attention to three areas of social values. These are religion, morality and politics.

The question I was interested in answering was whether the young unemployed regard themselves as attributing more or less value to religion, politics or morality than those who have not been unemployed. Their replies clearly indicated that the experience of unemployment is not related to the worth ascribed to any of these areas.

Of these three social values, moral values are the most important to the young people and religious values are the least important. Thus, 81% of the young Centymca members claimed that moral values are important to them, compared with 47% who claimed that politics is important to them and 32% who claimed that religion is important to them. What precisely the young people meant by these claims will be explored in greater detail in subsequent sections.

BELIEFS

This section on beliefs turns attention to the relationship between the experience of unemployment and the young person's religious beliefs and attitudes. An examination of this relationship is of particular importance and interest for two reasons. There is a very practical reason for examining this area, and also an interesting theoretical reason.

The practical reason is this. The churches are trying to respond to the problems of unemployment by exploring the ways in which church initiative can help to alleviate the impact of unemployment. It is for this reason that the 'Church Action with the Unemployed' campaign was established and began to make itself widely known at the beginning of 1982, under the chairmanship of the Reverend Canon Frank Scuffham, the industrial chaplain to Corby. In order to respond effectively to the needs of the young unemployed the churches need to listen carefully to what the young unemployed are themselves saying about religion.

In addition to this practical objective, there is also a very interesting theoretical problem implied in the literature on the psychology of religion into the possible relationships between unemployment and religion. The nature of this theoretical problem is suggested by books such as Michael Argyle and Benjamin Beit-Hallahmi's review published in 1975, The Social Psychology of Religion, about the various theories advanced to explain the place and importance of religion. For example, on the one hand it might be argued that religion is an expression of dependency needs. In the light of this argument, if the unemployed are indeed under greater personal pressure and personal threat, we might well expect them to need to turn more frequently to religion for support. On the other hand, it might be argued that religion is an expression of social conformity. In the light of this argument, if the unemployed are indeed inclined to feel themselves to be more alienated from society, we might well expect them to project some of their feelings of alienation into a stronger rejection of religion.

So much, then, for conflicting theories: what does the evidence of the survey itself tend to suggest? Interestingly, it supports aspects of both theories, depending, of course, on what is taken as an index of religious belief.

To begin with, the young unemployed are more likely to reject the social and public signs of religious belief. This means that they are likely to have less time for the church and less contact with the churches. An indication of this tendency is provided by the proportions of the young members of the Centymca Club who claim to attend church. 16% of the long-term unemployed said that they had been to a place of worship within the past month, compared with 20% of the short-term unemployed and 21% of the those young people who had no recent experience of unemployment.

The tendency for the young people who have been out of work to have less contact with the churches is also reflected in their greater tendency to reject what the churches are seen to stand for. 17% of the young people who had been unemployed claimed to be atheists who rejected all possibility of belief in God, compared with 13% of those who had not been unemployed. 21% of the young people who had been unemployed firmly rejected the central Christian belief that Jesus Christ is the Son of God, compared with 17% of those who had not been unemployed. Similarly, 25% of the long-term unemployed rejected the possibility of life after death, compared with 18% of those who had no recent experience of unemployment.

Along with this greater rejection of God, Jesus, life after death and the church, so the unemployed young people are also less likely to have any time for the bible. In fact, bible reading itself is practised by very few young people nowadays, but it seems to be practised even less by those who had been out of work than by those who had not been unemployed. Thus, only 7% of the long-term unemployed claimed to have looked at a bible within the past month, compared with 10% of those who had no recent experience of unemployment.

The greater antipathy of the unemployed towards religion is reflected also in their attitude towards the provision of religious education in schools. As a whole, the young members of the Centymca Club did not feel strongly against the provision of religious education in school. Overall, 58% of the young people were in favour of religious education and 27% were uncertain about the priority they would give to it, leaving only about three in every twenty who were positively against it. However, the proportion who expressed positive disapproval vis à vis the place of religious education in schools were very clearly related to their employment history. 22% of the long-term unemployed argued that religious education should not be taught in schools, compared with 16% of the short-term unemployed and between 13% and 14% of those who had no recent experience of unemployment.

Given the impact of all this cumulative evidence to support the notion that the young people who have been out of work feel themselves more alienated from the public aspects of religion, it is a matter of considerable surprise to find that the young unemployed actually profess a greater dependence upon the personal and private practice of religion. It is in fact the case that the young unemployed are much more likely than their employed contemporaries to turn to the private practice of prayer. Thus, 39% of the long-term unemployed admitted that they had prayed by themselves within the last week and so did 34% of the short-term unemployed. Only 29% of the young people who have no recent experience of unemployment claimed to have prayed within the past week.

The replies to the Centymca Attitude Inventory therefore seem to indicate that the experience of unemployment is related to the young person's religious beliefs and religious attitudes in two distinct senses. On the one hand, the young people who have experienced unemployment are more likely to want to reject the belief in God and the church. At the same time, they are more likely actually to need to turn to God for support through prayer.

This chapter has attempted to interpret the unemployed young person's more frequent use of personal prayer as an indication of dependency needs. If this is the case, then we might well expect the unemployed young people to turn more frequently to other external sources of help as well. This is precisely what happens, for example, in relationship to their belief in their horoscopes. Whereas 51% of the young people who had no recent experience of unemployment clearly rejected belief in horoscopes, this proportion fell to 46% of the short-term unemployed and 42% of the long-term unemployed. In this sense, the young unemployed are more inclined to find themselves grasping at straws of hope and possibilities of support. Interestingly, just as their greater dependence on prayer is not reflected in a greater belief in God, neither is their greater use of horoscopes reflected in a greater belief in the way in which luck actually affects their lives. Fundamentally, the unemployed are not more superstitious than the employed, just more desperate for any source of help which may prove to be useful or supportive.

Before leaving this discussion of the relationship between the experience of unemployment and religion, there is one further issue which it is worthwhile to explore. This is the complicated issue of the triangular relationship between unemployment and suicide, between religion and suicide, and between unemployment and religion. Durkheim's early study on Suicide, published in 1897, drew attention to the idea that, in some senses, religious affiliation reduces suicidal tendencies. In more recent years the problem has been discussed by psychologists like Benjamin Beit-Hallahmi writing in the journal Psychological Reports for 1975, Steven Stack writing in the journal Social Psychiatry in 1980 and Jon Hoelter writing in the journal Suicide and Life-Threatening Behaviour for 1979.

The point of immediate interest for our present study is that Chapter 4 has already confirmed that the young unemployed in the present sample were more likely to entertain suicidal thoughts than the young employed, while the present chapter has indicated ways in which religious beliefs and the public practice of religion may well have a lower hold on the young unemployed. Is there a way, then, in which the group of young people most likely to be in danger of suicidal activity are also the least likely to be in touch with the inhibiting influences of religion?

In order to provide some indication on this vexed issue, the Centymca Attitude Inventory included the simple question 'I think suicide is a sin'. Significantly less of the young unemployed were likely to think in terms of suicide being a sin than was the case among the young employed. Thus, 50% of the long-term unemployed positively disagreed with the notion that suicide is a sin, compared with 47% of the short-term unemployed and 45% of those who had no recent history of unemployment. In this way, it seems that the long-term unemployed are both more likely to entertain suicidal thoughts and less likely to be inhibited by religious beliefs from implementing these thoughts in terms of either successful or unsuccessful suicide attempts.

7. Morals and Law

MORALS

The purpose of this section is to turn attention to the question of moral beliefs and attitudes. Morality came very much to the forefront in the discussion of the values of young people during the 1960s and early 1970s. Indeed, the changing face of moral standards became one of the touchstones by which the prevailing trends of the culture of young people were described. In this way, Daniel Yankelovich found it appropriate to give the title The New Morality to the profile of 'American Youth in the 1970s' which he published in 1974. The area of morals remains one of central importance both to young people themselves and to those working with them.

What, then, are the prevailing moral attitudes of young people as they enter the 1980s? How sure are they about their moral views? How liberal are they in their outlook on moral matters? Do the young people who have had the experience of being out of work regard moral issues any differently from those who have not had the misfortune of experiencing unemployment?

In order to sample the moral attitudes of the young members of the Centymca Club over a range of issues, I decided to select three main areas of morality for inclusion in the Centymca Attitude Inventory. The first of these three areas concerned sexual ethics, including the young person's attitude towards contraception, marriage, sex outside marriage and the practice of homosexuality. Secondly, I decided to look at the young person's attitude towards the sanctity of human life, by concentrating on issues concerning life and death, like abortion, euthanasia and war. Thirdly, I was interested in assessing their attitudes towards alcohol abuse and towards the use of drugs.

Sex

The discussion of values in Chapter 6 has already drawn attention to the fact that the vast majority of young people regard moral values to be important to them. This does not mean that young people are holding the traditional moral norms of society in high regard. It means that their own moral code is one which they take seriously and about which they are quite clear.

It is particularly the case in the area of sexual morality that the sixteeen to twenty-five year olds have made up their minds where they stand. In answer to the questions in this area in the Centymca Attitude Inventory very few of them indeed choose the 'not certain' category of response.

The liberalisation of heterosexual ethics among young people is now well established. The period of indecision is over. Only a very small proportion of the sixteen to twenty-five year olds adopted a conservative attitude towards heterosexual ethics. For example, only 3% believed that contraception is wrong. Similarly, only 6% believed that it is wrong for an ummarried couple to live together and 10% said that they believed it is wrong to have sexual intercourse outside marriage. The vast majority of them accepted these practices as morally right. Moreover, about two-thirds of those who accepted these practices as morally right felt strongly about their acceptance of them.

Given this fairly clear consensus regarding the attitudes of young people to matters of heterosexual morality, it is perhaps hardly surprising that there was no significant difference in the views expressed on these matters by the young people who had experienced unemployment and those who had not. The experience of unemployment is an insignificant factor in relationship to such well established prevailing moral norms.

However, when attention is turned from the discussion of heterosexual morality to the matter of homosexuality, quite a different pattern emerges. To begin with, the young people as a whole did not adopt such an unequivocally liberal view towards the practice of homosexuality. This was reflected through the responses to the Centymca Attitude Inventory in two ways. First, overall a much higher proportion of the young people declared the opinion that they considered homosexuality to be plainly wrong.

This view was held by 25% of the young members of the Centymca Club. Secondly, there was also a greater indecision among the young people on the homosexual question than on the heterosexual question. Whereas only 9% of the young people had not made up their minds about contraception and only 6% had not made up their minds about extra marital cohabitation, 18% of them had not made up their minds about homosexuality.

There is plainly a much greater variation in the views of young people about the morality of homosexual relationships than about the morality of heterosexual relationships. Consequently, it becomes particularly interesting to examine whether this greater variation in views permits more of a distinction to be identified between the moral attitudes of those who have experienced unemployment and those who have not had this experience. The analysis of the replies to the Centymca Attitude Inventory shows quite clearly that those young people who had been out of work tended to adopt a more liberal attitude towards the practice of homosexuality. Thus, 66% of those who had experienced unemployment refused to condemn the practice of homosexuality as wrong, compared with only 55% of those who had no recent experience of unemployment. This suggests that there might be a tendency towards a greater moral liberalism among the young who are unemployed.

Life and Death

Next, we turn attention to the three questions concerned with the sanctity of life. The first of them is the very broad issue to do with the justification of war. A high proportion of the young people, 61% of them, considered that all war is wrong. Moreover, nearly two-thirds of those who thought that all war is wrong felt strongly about the matter. This strong feeling may well reflect the strength of such movements as the Campaign for Nuclear Disarmament and the popular appeal of pacifism to today's young people. Again, the views of the unemployed young people do not differ on this issue from the views of their contemporaries who have not experienced unemployment.

The two key moral issues to do with the sanctity of human life concern abortion and euthanasia. The replies to the Centymca Attitude Inventory reveal that some interesting differences exist between the young person's responses to these two issues. Abortion is much more clearly acceptable to the young than euthanasia. The young find it less objectionable to contemplate the termination of a life which is not yet self-supporting than the termination of a mature life, apparently even if that life is threatened by infirmity and suffering. Whereas 69% approved abortion as morally acceptable, only 46% approved euthanasia as morally acceptable. There was also considerably more uncertainty about the issue of euthanasia: 30% had not yet made up their minds about euthanasia, compared with 17% who had not yet made up their minds about abortion. On balance, 14% thought abortion is definitely wrong and 24% thought euthanasia is definitely wrong.

The young people's replies to these two central issues concerning abortion and euthanasia provide us with another opportunity to test whether the moral attitudes of the young people who had experienced unemployment differ from those who have not had this experience. Once again, the unemployed emerge as holding clearly more liberal moral views than their contemporaries who had not experienced unemployment. Thus, 74% of those young people who had experienced unemployment rejected the notion that abortion is morally wrong, compared with 69% of those who had not experienced unemployment. Similarly, 50% of the young people who had experienced unemployment rejected the notion that euthanasia is morally wrong, compared with 46% of those who had not experienced unemployment.

Drugs and Alcohol

The final area examined in this section on morality evaluates the attitudes of young people towards alcohol and drugs. The two drugs singled out for attention are marijuana and heroin. Although the possession of both marijuana and heroin is illegal, the replies to these two questions indicate that young people make a clear distinction between the morality of the use of hard and soft drugs.

The vast majority of the young members of the Centymca Club considered that the use of a drug like heroin is morally wrong. Thus, 79% of the whole group came out clearly against the use of heroin, and a further 11% said that they had not made up their minds about the issue. This leaves only a minority, 10% of the young people, who were willing to support the use of heroin. Once again, in this situation of moral concensus, there is no significant difference in the attitudes of those who had experienced unemployment and those who had not.

On the issue of marijuana, however, there is a much greater diversity of moral opinion. Of the total sample of young people, 38% declared the view that the use of marijuana is morally wrong, while 43% declared the opposite view that the use of marijuana is morally right. This leaves a further 19% who had not made up their mind one way or the other. In this situation of a greater diversity of moral opinion, the analysis so far reviewed in the present chapter would lead us to suspect that the young people who had experienced unemployment would tend to hold a more liberal view towards the use of marijuana than those who had not experienced unemployment. The statistics from the Centymca Attitude Inventory support this hypothesis. 48% of the young people who had experienced unemployment refused to condemn the use of marijuana, compared with 42% of those who had not experienced unemployment.

The final question in this section, on the morality of drunkenness, is of particular interest in the exploration of the psychological correlates of unemployment. From Philip Eisenberg and Paul Lazarsfeld's early review of 'The Psychological Effects of Unemployment' published in the Psychological Bulletin in 1938, drinking has been indentified as one of the psychological escape mechanisms open to the unemployed. More recent attention to excessive alcohol intake among the unemployed has been given by Leonard Fagin's study of unemployment and health and the more specialist study of R G Smart into drinking problems among the unemployed and those employed as shift workers or in other capacities.

In the light of this history of research in the area of the relationship between unemployment and drinking, and also in the light of the greater moral liberalism of the unemployed identified in the present chapter, we might well expect the unemployed young people in the sample to be more tolerant of drunkenness. In fact the very opposite is the case. Whereas 29% of those who had not experienced unemployment considered that it is wrong to become drunk, this proportion rose to 31% among the short-term unemployed and 39% among the long-term unemployed. If there is a greater danger for the long-term unemployed to turn to alcohol as a way of drowning their sorrows, it seems that they also have a sharper perception of the dangers inherent in such a course of action.

LAW

The review of moral beliefs and attitudes in the previous section had drawn attention to the tendency of the young unemployed to adopt a somewhat more liberal stance in relationship to traditional moral absolutes than their employed contemporaries, at least in relationship to those issues which reflect a diversity of opinion among young people. One theory which could explain this tendency would speak in terms of the young unemployed feeling themselves to be more alienated from the society which imposes and gives sanction to these traditional moral absolutes. In this sense, the rejection of religion and the rejection of moral absolutes go hand in hand as part of the same alienation from society.

The purpose of the present section is to extend our review from religion and morality to an examination of the young person's attitude towards the law. If the same psychological dynamics apply to this area as to the previous two, we should expect that the young people who have been recently out of work will be found to adopt less law-abiding attitudes than those who had not experienced unemployment. After all, the law is a very clear symbol of the demands made by society upon the individual.

As a gentle way into sampling the young person's attitude towards the law, some items concerned with motoring offences were included in the Centymca Attitude Inventory. The most interesting of these asks the young people to respond to the sentence 'There is nothing wrong with drinking and driving if you can get away with it'. Their replies indicated that the extensive propaganda given to this issue has been highly successful. 89% of the sixteen to twenty-five year olds had no hesitation at all in rejecting this proposition and the majority of them, 60%, rejected it strongly. A further 6% of the young people said that they had not completely made up their minds on this issue. So this leaves just 5% of them who were willing to condone the breaking of the law by drinking and driving.

Like some of the issues reviewed in the section on morality, this question about drinking and driving reached such a consensus opinion among the young people that once again it is not all that surprising that there is no significant difference in the responses of those who had experienced unemployment and those who had not.

The results from other questions about the law included in the Centymca Attitude Inventory tend to support the hypothesis that the young unemployed feel more alienated from society than their employed contemporaries. For example, the tendency of the young unemployed to be less scrupulous in their attitude towards the law is especially evident in the areas concerned with money. The young people who have experienced unemployment are, quite naturally, generally much more short of cash than the young people who have not experienced unemployment. Consequently, they seem more willing to cut corners in order to save money where they can. An example of this is the way in which a higher proportion of the unemployed, especially the long-term unemployed, were willing to accept the notion that there is nothing wrong in travelling on public transport without buying a ticket, if you could get away with it. Thus, 25% of the long-term unemployed condoned this kind of behaviour, compared with 21% of the short-term unemployed and 19% of those who had no recent experience of unemployment. It seems likely that the long-term unemployed are having to think especially carefully about spending cash on things like their bus fares, and consequently they become more willing to take the risk of trying to get away without buying a ticket.

The next question tackles the issue of the way in which the young people perceive their responsibility to declare all earned income for the purposes of taxation. The particular interest behind this question concerns the so-called 'black economy'. It is often assumed that a lot of casual earnings go unassessed for taxation. Various writers have suggested that the unemployed might be particularly susceptible to infringing taxation requirements. Three reasons are advanced to support this notion. The unemployed are those who have the time, the opportunity and the greatest motivation for picking up casual earnings. The unemployed are those most likely to resent declaring small casual earnings for taxation when they feel that they need every penny that they can earn. But more seriously still, those drawing state benefits are strictly limited in the sum that they can legitimately earn before suffering reduction in their income provided by the state. The declaration of earned income for taxation purposes also implies declaration for the assessment of state allowances. According to this argument, the unemployed have greater incentive for failing to declare casual and untaxed earnings.

Having listened to the arguments advanced on this matter, what in fact are the views of young people on the issue of making dishonest tax returns to the Inland Revenue? Overall, just over half of the young members of the Centymca Club argued that tax returns should be filled in with complete honesty. This means that, on average, one young person in every two was willing to try to get away with giving incomplete or inaccurate information to the Inland Revenue, while the other young person in every two was not willing to do this.

Now, how is the attitude to this issue related to the experience of unemployment? The first point to emerge from the replies to the Centymca Attitude Inventory is that there is no difference in the proportion of the young people who had experienced short-term unemployment and those who had experienced no unemployment who argued that tax returns should be filled in with complete honesty. Between 53% and 54% of these two groups adopted this strictly law-abiding position. However, the second point to emerge is that the long-term unemployed were significantly more likely to condone the evasion of taxation than those who had either no experience of unemployment or only short-term experience of unemployment. The proportion of the long-term unemployed who argued that tax returns should be filled in with complete honesty fell to 47%.

The final question in this section focuses on the issue of the willingness of sixteen to twenty-five year olds to condone the sale of cigarettes to children under the legal age. This kind of question is particularly interesting because it is a matter of only a recently short space of time since these young people were themselves technically restricted in their access to tobacco by the law. In retrospect, how much do young people resent restrictions imposed upon them as minors, and how much do they value these restrictions as having been for their own good?

Overall, a surprisingly high proportion of these sixteen to twenty-five year olds were in favour of the enforcement of the restrictions on the sale of cigarettes to children under the legal age. 84% of the young members of the Centymca Club actually declared that they thought it is wrong to sell cigarettes to children under the legal age. This is a much higher proportion of the young people than those who condemned travelling without a ticket, the breaking of speed limits or the violation of parking restrictions. The consensus opinion seems to accept that, in cases like this, the law is right in restricting the freedom of children until they come of age to make mature and responsible decisions for themselves.

The final point that needs to be noticed, however, is that on this issue, even when there seems to be a general consensus of opinion among young people, the unemployed tend to be less in favour of the enforcement of the law than those who have no recent experience of unemployment. In this way, 80% of the long-term unemployed and 81% of the short-term unemployed condemn the sale of cigarettes to children under the legal age, compared with 86% of those who had no recent experience of unemployment.

8. Politics and Society

POLITICS

The research from the 1930s on the relationship between unemployment and political attitudes produced conflicting conclusions. In their attempt to summarise this research in 1938, Philip Eisenberg and Paul Lazarsfeld draw attention to some writers who conclude that unemployment leads to greater political radicalism, while others suggest that unemployment may function in an entirely different direction and engender greater sympathy for fascism. The lack of clarity to emerge from these 1930s studies makes it difficult for us to advance a sensible hypothesis about the relationship between unemployment and political attitudes on the basis of previous research alone.

Moreover, there are three other reasons why it might be unwise to advance predictions about the political implications of umemployment from these early studies. First, the evidence quoted from the 1930s is mainly American in origin. Second, the political climate and even the meaning of political concepts is quite different in the 1980s from the situation in the 1930s. Third, in a recent paper in the Bulletin of the British Psychological Society under the title 'Research on Unemployment: Defects, Neglect and Prospects', the authors (Ross Gurney of the Department of Employment and Youth Affairs, Canberra, Australia and Keith Taylor) caution the relevance of results from the early studies for interpreting the contemporary psychological impact of unemployment on the ground that 'research in the 1930s appears to have been insufficiently rigorous, may have lost relevance because of changes in the phenomena being studied and in the surrounding social conditions, did not make sharp enough conceptual distinctions, and was not as extensive as is sometimes thought'. Against this background, it is wise to approach the examination of the political correlates of unemployment among young people in the 1980s with an open mind.

The earlier section on values indicated that 47% of the young members of the Centymca Club claimed that politics is important to them. The first purpose of the present section is to explore what they mean by this claim. To what extent do the sixteen to twenty-five year olds actually take an active part in politics? To what extent have they made up their minds on key political issues? What in fact are the political attitudes and values which the majority of young people are espousing? And, most important of all, to what extent are the answers to these questions related to the young person's experience of unemployment?

In order to answer these questions the Centymca Attitude Inventory included three main sets of items. The first set is concerned with the interest and active involvement which young people show in politics, the confidence they place in the party political system through which the country is governed, and their attitude towards the policies of the major political parties which engage in that system. The second set is concerned with the young person's attitudes on a series of key specific political issues. The aim here is to assess the extent to which they have formulated views on certain political matters and the extent to which their attitudes are of a consistent political persuasion across different issues. The third set is concerned with the politics of wages and the relative social worth of different occupational groups, ranging from manual workers to professional people.

Although nearly half of the young members of the Centymca Club claimed that politics is important to them, only a very small proportion, slightly less than 8% of the total membership, actually takes an active part in politics. What is especially interesting, however, is that there is a greater tendency for the young people who had experienced long-term unemployment to take an active part in politics than for other young people. 12% of the long-term unemployed said that they took an active part in politics, compared with 7% of the other young people. Moreover, there is no significant difference in the proportions of the short-term unemployed and those who had not experienced unemployment in their response to this question. It seems that, instead of leading to increased apathy towards politics, the experience of long-term unemployment tends to encourage the young people to believe that a political solution could have a positive effect on their situation, and this encourages them to become more politically active.

Overall, the young people included in this survey do not seem to have a large degree of confidence or faith in the British party political system. 27% of the total sample said that they did not consider that it really makes any difference at all which political party is in power. While not actively agreeing with this sentiment, a further 22% of the sample remained sceptical as to whether they could expect any real differences to emerge from a change of government. This means that only half of the sixteen to twenty-five year olds questioned had confidence that there is some real point in the political choice offered to them at the polling station.

A similar conclusion emerges from an analysis of the proportion of the young people who expressed confidence in the policies of one of the major political parties. Exactly 50% of the young people said that they tended to support one of the major political parties when it comes to election time. This means that half of the young members of the Centymca Club are the floating voters who do not have consistent confidence in any of the major political parties.

Just as the long-term unemployed were more likely to claim to take an active part in politics, so they were more likely to express confidence in the idea that the choice of government is an important factor in determining the shape of things. Only 23% of the long-term unemployed dismissed politics on the grounds that it makes no difference which political party is in power, compared with 31% of the short-term unemployed and 29% of the those who had no recent experience of unemployment.

The climate of political opinion is a changing phenomenon. It is for this reason that the major political parties find it necessary to take frequent soundings of their status in public opinion through regular national opinion polls. It is for this reason, too, that a democratic country experiences a regular pendulum swing in the political colour of the party which holds government as a direct indication of changes in the majority political persuasion of the electorate. It is problematic, therefore, to know how to interpret the proportions of young people claiming to support the different political parties when the data have been collected over a lengthy period of time, as is the case in the present study. Moreover, from the perspective of contemporary political predictions, there is one major weakness in the present data. The data collection was initiated immediately prior to the official formation of the Social Democratic Party. As a consequence, the original version of the Centymca Attitude Inventory includes mention of the Conservative party, the Labour party and the Liberal party, and it was thought impractical to change the format of the questionnaire employed in this study during the lengthy period of its use.

In spite of these drawbacks, a lot can still be learnt by examining the relative support given by the employed and the unemployed to the three major political parties included in the Centymca Attitude Inventory, rather than from concentrating on the absolute levels of support given to each party. What we learn from this kind of analysis is that there are no major differences in the level of support given to the Conservative party, the Labour party or the Liberal party by the short-term unemployed and by those who had no recent experience of unemployment.

Where the significant difference in political allegiance occurred was between the long-term unemployed and the rest of the sample. To begin with, significantly less of the long-term unemployed gave their support to the Conservative party. The long-term unemployed showed greater disaffection to the Conservative party. It is interesting to see the direction in which the allegiance of the long-term unemployed is transferred in order to compensate for the loss of confidence in the Conservative party. The political allegiance of the long-term unemployed was not transferred to the Labour party. The Labour party received support from the same proportion of the long-term unemployed, the short-term unemployed and those who had no recent experience of unemployment. This political allegiance was being transferred to the Liberal party. Thus, the Liberal party received support from 13% of the long-term unemployed, compared with 8% of the short-term unemployed and 7% of those who had not recently been out of work.

The next batch of questions to be analysed turned attention to the attitudes of the young people towards certain key political issues. The overall impression gained from the replies to these questions was that there is a predominantly right wing mood among the sixteen to twenty-five year old members of the Centymca Club. Generally speaking, the young people tended not to be in favour of state control of industry, education or medicine. The young people seemed to be speaking clearly in favour of private enterprise. Thus, only 20% actively favoured the nationalisation of industry, compared with 41% who spoke against it. Only 12% supported the abolition of private schools, compared with 71% who felt uneasy about this kind of state monopoly. Similarly, only 15% supported the suppression of private medical practice, compared with 65% who felt that it is right to preserve this kind of freedom of choice for the medical practitioner and for the patient.

The fact that a lower proportion of the long-term unemployed said that they supported the policies of the Conservative party might lead us to suspect that there would be a lower level of support for the protection of private enterprise among the long-term unemployed. However, the fact that there is no greater support for the Labour party among the long-term unemployed would, at the same time, lead us to be cautious about this prediction. What, then, do the replies of the long-term unemployed to the three specific items about the state control of industry, education and medicine tell us?

The answer to this question is not a completely straightforward one. While the long-term unemployed did show a greater support for the state control of education, they did not show greater support for the state control of industry or medicine. Perhaps, there is a greater tendency for the long-term unemployed to feel that those educated in private schools have an unfair advantage in the employment stakes and for this reason they are more likely to want to see the suppression of private schools. On the other hand, they did not seem to feel that the nationalisation of industry was likely to create a more successful industrial environment or more jobs; the issue of private medicine is probably irrelevant to the employment situation anyway. The development of left wing attitudes in the long-term unemployed seems to be directly related to their understanding of the employment situation.

If it is true that the unemployed are likely to adopt less right wing attitudes on political questions which are directly

related to the employment situation, then we would expect
the unemployed to give more support to the trade unions.
One of the roles that trade unions see themselves as
adopting is the preservation of the jobs of their members
against the redundancies induced by re-organisation,
rationalisation, mechanisation and productivity deals. The
replies of the young people to the Centymca Attitude
Inventory confirmed this expectation. While the majority of
the young people were critical of the power wielded by the
trade unions, there was less criticism voiced by the
unemployed. Thus, 65% of the long-term unemployed and
68% of the short-term unemployed said that they thought
the trade unions have too much power, compared with 72%
of those who had no recent experience of unemployment.

It might have been expected that the unemployed would
become more protective of the home economy than those
whose employment prospects were more secure. In fact,
the very reverse of this is the case. For example, instead
of trying to protect jobs by placing more restrictions on
immigration, the long-term unemployed as a group were less
sympathetic towards immigration restrictions. Of the
long-term unemployed 23% argued that there should be no
restrictions on immigration into Britain, compared with 19%
of the short-term unemployed and 18% of those who had no
recent experience of unemployment. Similarly, instead of
feeling a greater need to support home industry in order to
encourage work, the long-term unemployed felt less inclined
to buy British. Thus, only 12% of the long-term
unemployed said that they would rather buy a British car
than one made in another country, compared with 15% of the
short-term unemployed and 18% of the employed.

Another political question gauges the young person's
response to the European Economic Community. Their
replies indicated that there was much more support for the
European Economic Community among the young members of
the Centymca Club than hostility towards it. 44% of them
considered that the Common Market is a good thing,
compared with 16% who did not think it is a good thing.
These statistics also imply that two-fifths of the young
people had not made up their minds what they think of the
Common Market. Moreover, there was no great difference
in the perceptions of the employed and the unemployed on
this issue.

The final batch of questions in this section tapped the political awareness and values of young people by selecting a variety of jobs which have different functions or status in society and by asking the respondents to assess whether the people doing these jobs were being adequately paid for their work or not. The five main employment categories included in the survey range from manual workers to professional people. They are doctors, nurses, policemen, car workers and miners.

The job which the young people most clearly regarded as underpaid was that of the nurse. 75% of the young members of the Centymca Club thought that nurses should be paid more. Next, 56% regarded doctors as being underpaid. Very closely behind doctors came policemen, with 53% regarding the police as underpaid. The young people appeared to place a high value on those working on behalf of society - both in health care and in the maintenance of law and order. On the other hand, they had much less concern for those in the industries which they regard as having greater bargaining power in relationship to salary. Only 7% thought that car workers were underpaid, and 26% were concerned that miners were underpaid for the job they do.

Interestingly, the experience of unemployment bears no relationship to the way in which young people evaluate the pay claims of nurses, policemen, car workers or miners. The only significant relationship between unemployment and the young person's response to any of the questions in this section concerned the evaluation of doctors. Only 48% of the long-term unemployed thought that doctors were underpaid for the job they do, compared with 58% of those who had had no recent experience of unemployment. This indicates a lower regard for the higher paid professionals among those who are themselves least well off.

SOCIETY

This section on society examines the attitudes of the young people towards specific features of the world in which they live. What do young people think about the society in which they are growing up? To what extent are they concerned about the major issues which affect that society?

Are they disturbed by their perceptions of the way in which society is moving? What are their priorities for social change? Do the young unemployed feel differently about these matters from the young people who have had no recent experience of unemployment? Does the experience of unemployment tend to make them more radical in their attitudes towards society or more apathetic in their response to the world situation?

The Centymca Attitude Inventory attempts to assess the young person's attitude towards society by concentrating on three types of questions. The first batch of questions examines the extent to which young people feel that society is going down hill. It is concerned with an assessment of the level of their pessimism regarding the direction of social trends and the prospects for the future. The second batch of questions concentrates specifically on what might be called the moral climate of society. It asks young people to evaluate the moral implications of social trends. The third batch of questions moves onto a wider front to look at the seriousness with which the young people take some of the major issues confronting the world today.

Views on Social Trends

The overall impression gained from the responses of the young members of the Centymca Club to the first batch of questions was that their basic view of life in Britain was both depressing and pessimistic. The majority of the young people seemed to consider themselves to be living in a declining and decaying society. They felt that around them things seemed to be getting worse. The three central indications of this mood are provided by the young person's perceptions of what is happening to the crime rate, the health service and the educational system.

To begin with, a large majority of the young people felt that the society in which they were living was becoming less safe. 73% of the young members of the Centymca Club shared the perception that the crime rate is rising, compared with only 4% who positively rejected this perception as not ringing true for them. Listening to the news, reading the newspapers, and their own personal observations all seemed to add up to form this consensus of opinion.

These young persons' experience of school were still very recent in their minds. Some had only just left school, while the oldest could not have been away from school for more than ten years, even if they left school at the earliest possible opportunity. Many of them would have lived through some radical changes and reorganisations in the educational system. Their perceptions of what was happening in schools are, therefore, worth taking seriously. A large majority of them felt that the education provided by schools is deteriorating: 63% of the young members of the Centymca Club shared the perception that the educational standard of schools is declining, compared with only 14% who positively rejected this perception as not ringing true for them.

The development of the health service had been an important symbol of the progress which has transformed the quality of life for twentieth century Britain. Now, however, it is clear that a large proportion of the young people felt that the provision of the health service is seriously on the wane. Thus, 58% of the young members of the Centymca Club shared the perception that the health service is becoming more inefficient, compared with only 14% who positively rejected this perception as not ringing true for them.

Public safety, health and education are three aspects of life we tend to take for granted in the reconstruction of post-war Britain. The predominantly pessimistic attitudes, which the young people were taking on these three issues, bode ill for their perceptions of the society in which they were growing up and which their own lives and attitudes would help to form. Whether their perceptions of these social trends were objectively right or wrong is a comparatively unimportant question. The really significant thing is that perceptions of this sort can have a self-fulfilling quality. If you really believe that things are bad, before long you will begin to make them so.

So far we have only examined the responses of the whole group of young people to these issues. Did the perceptions of the young people who had been out of work differ in any way on these issues from the perceptions of those who had not been unemployed? The answer is that the perceptions of the two groups did not significantly differ. The unemployed were neither more nor less pessimistic about these trends in society than those who had no recent experience of unemployment.

Given this pessimistic approach to life in today's society, what future did the young people actually see for Britain? It is here that the long-term unemployed were seen to take a significantly more pessimistic stance than their contemporaries who had either not experienced unemployment at all or who had experienced only short-term unemployment. Of the long-term unemployed, 31% flatly concluded that they did not see much future for Britain at all, compared with 22% of the short-term unemployed and 23% of those who had no recent experience of unemployment.

Views on Moral Trends

The overall impression gained from the responses of the young members of the Centymca Club to the second batch of questions is that the majority opinion supported most of the changes that are taking place in the liberalisation of society's attitude towards issues of morality. Considerable changes have taken place in the moral climate of society during the relatively short space of time covered by the lives of these young people. Generally speaking, they seemed to feel that these changes are making the world a better, rather than a worse, place in which to live. This mood was reflected in the young person's attitude towards social changes affecting abortion, divorce and television. It did not, however, extend to include their attitudes towards pornography and credit facilities. On these two latter issues the majority opinion of the young people tended to feel that society is making things unnecessarily difficult for itself.

As far as abortion is concerned, 25% of the young members of the Centymca Club considered that society had made it too easy to have an abortion, compared with 51% who did not consider this to be the case. As far as divorce is concerned, 29% of the young members of the Centymca Club considered that society has made it too easy to get a divorce, compared with 44% who did not consider this to be the case. 32% of the young members of the Centymca Club were critical of the amount of violence screened on television, but a higher proportion (43%) were

not critical of the way in which television censorship has
been progressively relaxed over the past years.

A different picture emerges, however, in relationship to
the young person's perception of pornography and credit
facilities. The majority opinion believed that pornography
is now too readily available. Thus, 43% of the young
people were critical of the open display of pornography,
compared with 32% who did not feel that society has
overstepped the mark on this issue. The majority opinion
also believed that credit facilities have become too readily
available and encourage people to build up unnecessary and
crippling debts. Thus, 45% of the young people were
critical of credit facilities, compared with 33% who did not
feel that this is causing a social problem.

The earlier section on morals would lead us to suspect
that the young people who had been out of work would tend
to adopt a more radical or permissive attitude towards the
moral climate of society. Their responses to the questions
concerning social trends affecting abortion and divorce
confirmed this hypothesis. The unemployed were more
likely to dismiss criticism of social trends in abortion and
divorce than those who had no recent experience of
unemployment. For example, 59% of the long-term
unemployed and 59% of the short-term unemployed rejected
the criticism that it is becoming too easy to obtain an
abortion, compared with 50% of those who had no recent
experience of unemployment. 55% of the long-term
unemployed and 48% of the short-term unemployed rejected
the criticism that it is becoming too easy to obtain a
divorce, compared with 41% of those who had no recent
experience of unemployment.

On the other hand, our hypothesis is contradicted by the
responses to the questions concerning social trends in
credit facilities and television. It was the long-term
unemployed who were much more critical about the impact of
easy credit facilities on society. 51% of the long-term
unemployed argued that the credit card encourages careless
spending, compared with 43% of the short-term unemployed
and 45% of those who had no recent experience of
unemployment. In this case, it seems that the financial
stringencies of long-term unemployment were more important
in determining the attitudes of the unemployed than their
feelings of moral radicalism. Chapter 7 has already drawn

attention to the way in which the long-term unemployed
were more likely to be worried by debts. It is totally
understandable, then, why they should be more inclined to
be critical of the society which helps them to spend beyond
their means.

The unemployed were also more critical of the amount of
violence shown on television. 40% of the long-term
unemployed and 40% of the short-term unemployed felt that
there is too much violence on television, compared with 29%
of those who had no recent experience of unemployment.
Perhaps this difference is explicable in terms of the
hypothesis that the unemployed had allowed themselves to
become more exposed to what is shown on television, and
therefore reacted more strongly against it.

Views on World Issues

The overall impression gained from the responses of the
young people at the Centymca Club to the third batch of
questions in this section is that the majority of young
people demonstrated a considerable degree of concern about
the problems which are thought to be major issues
confronting today's society. They seemed to be aware of
what is going on in the world and to take their awareness
seriously.

The Centymca Attitude Inventory listed six problems
which face the world today. The order of priority which
the young people gave to these problems placed the issue of
environmental pollution at the top of their list. Pollution
was followed by inflation, homelessness, unemployment,
nuclear war and the Third World. Thus, 85% were
concerned about the risk of pollution to the environment;
82% were concerned about the rate of inflation; 78% were
concerned about the problems of homelessness; 74% were
concerned about the problems of unemployment; 73% were
concerned about the risks of nuclear war; 69% were
concerned about the poverty of the Third World. These
percentages demonstrate that the young people are most
concerned about issues likely to affect them personally, like
the question of pollution, and least concerned about those
that are furthest away, like the Third World.

The attitudes of the young people who had experienced
unemployment did not differ from those who had not

shared that experience in relationship to the concern they showed for issues like pollution, homelessness, nuclear war or the Third World. The two areas in which the level of concern registered by the employed and the unemployed differed were both much more closely related to the experience of unemployment itself.

The comparison of the way in which the long-term unemployed, the short-term unemployed and the employed rated their level of concern about the problems of unemployment itself is very interesting. The short-term unemployed were much more concerned about the problems of unemployment than those who had no experience of unemployment. However, the long-term unemployed registered a lower level of concern about the problems of unemployment than the level registered by those who had no recent experience of unemployment. Thus, 80% of the short-term unemployed said that they are concerned about the problems of unemployment, compared with 73% of those who had no recent experience of unemployment and 69% of the long-term unemployed. Those who had experienced long-term unemployment seemed to have become hardened to the issue and no longer rated it so highly as a matter of concern.

The comparison of the way in which the long-term unemployed, the short-term unemployed and the employed rated their level of concern about inflation is also very interesting. The employed and the short-term unemployed both agreed in the importance they attribute to this problem, while the long-term unemployed once again attributed less significance to the issue. Thus, only 74% of the long-term unemployed said that they are concerned with the rate of inflation, compared with 83% of the short-term unemployed and 82% of those who had no recent experience of unemployment. As the financial stringencies of long-term unemployment begin to bite harder, so it seems that the long-term unemployed may become less aware of, and less concerned about, the impact of inflation upon prices and the purchasing power of the money in their pockets.

9. Work and Leisure

WORK

The re-entry into work after periods of unemployment
rarely goes smoothly. There are a number of reasons for
this. When unemployment has damaged the young person's
self concept and confidence, a lot of ground has to be made
up before work reassumes its normal significance in their
lives. Meanwhile, the new job can seem particularly
threatening and worrying. When the young person has
been unemployed for some time, their rhythm of life settles
down to a different pace and they cease to be accustomed
to the regular pattern of working hours. During the
period of readjustment, they can feel very tired and
pressurised. When people have been out of work, it is not
uncommon for them to lose their confidence to be able to
cope with the job itself and with the human relationships
that go with it.

Another important point is that the young people who
have experienced unemployment often feel that they have
had little option about the job they finally succeed in
securing for themselves. Many may well end up in
situations which they would never have dreamed of
accepting, had the employment market been more favourable
to them. It is much more difficult to enter the job of one's
choice from the situation of unemployment than it is from
the situation of already being employed.

Against this background of theory, it becomes important
to assess the extent to which those who have experienced
unemployment are deriving satisfaction from the jobs which
they have recently entered, and how their level of
satisfaction compares with that of the young people who
have not come from a background of recent unemployment.

The first question in this section assesses the proportion
of young people who reported that they are unhappy in
their work. 12% of the young people who had experienced
unemployment said that they are now working in a job

in which they are totally unhappy, compared with 8% of the young people who had not experienced unemployment. Those who had returned to work after experiencing long-term unemployment were not more likely to be unhappy in their work than those returning after experiencing only short-term unemployment.

Although long-term unemployment does not appear to cause more damage than short-term unemployment to the young person's happiness in the job to which they are eventually appointed, long-term unemployment does have a significantly more damaging impact than short-term unemployment on the young person's ability to establish effective relationships with new work mates. As a rule, the majority of young people seemed willing to make the most of the people with whom they find themselves working. 86% of the young people who had not experienced unemployment said that they like the people they work with. Those who had experienced short-term unemployment were less likely to feel so positively about their work mates, and yet 81% still agreed that they like the people they work with. Where the real difference comes is in the response to this question among the long-termed unemployed: only 71% found their work mates likeable.

The long-term unemployed were also least likely to cope with the demands of re-entry into work. This is indicated, for example, by the increase in their tendency to worry about their work. It is not uncommon for young people in this age group to report that their work is a real source of worry, but certainly the young people most likely to report this situation were those who had re-entered work after a lengthy period of unemployment. While 44% of those who had no experience of unemployment and 44% of those who had short-term experience of unemployment said that they often worry about their work, this proportion rises to 54% of those with long-term experience of unemployment.

Another indication of the lower satisfaction which those who had experienced long-term unemployment derive from their new work is given by the proportion of young people who said that they frequently wish they could change their job. Among those who had not experienced unemployment, 26% felt this way about their present work. 27% of those who had short-term experience of unemployment felt this way as well. Then the proportion rises to 32% of those who had long-term experience of unemployment.

One of the key problems often aired among those discussing youth unemployment is the extent to which the young unemployed may be to some extent self-selected. While it is now well appreciated that the employment situation is such that many young people who genuinely want to work are suffering enforced unemployment, the suspicion still lingers that some young people would actually rather be unemployed than out at work. The present survey included several questions to explore different aspects of this problem.

First of all, the young people were asked how important their work was to them. 89% of the young members of the Centymca Club replied that work is important to them, and replies to this question were in no ways related to their experience of unemployment. The young people who had been unemployed did not differ from those who had not been unemployed in the importance they attribute to work.

Next, an assessment was made of the young person's sense of ambition to do well at work. Their replies show that a higher proportion of the young people who had been unemployed wanted to do well at work, not a lower proportion of them. Thus, 85% of the long-term unemployed replied that they want to get to the top in their work, compared with 79% of those who had not been unemployed.

While the long-term unemployed claimed to be more ambitious, they were not, however, quite as committed to the importance of hard work in their lives as those who had never experienced unemployment. 84% of those who had experienced unemployment considered that it is important to work hard, compared with 88% of those who had not experienced unemployment.

The really revealing question on this issue of the relationship between attitudes towards work and the experience of unemployment has been left to last in the analysis afforded by this section. The young people were asked to rate their level of agreement with the direct question 'I would rather go on social security than get a job I don't like doing'. 15% of the young people who had no recent experience of unemployment replied that they felt this way about work. The proportion of young people who agreed with this notion, however, rose to 24% of those with

short-term experience of unemployment and 27% of those
with long-term experience of unemployment.   It seems,
then, that there might be an element of self-selection among
the young people who find themselves unemployed.   This
observation must not be taken to imply that all unemployed
young people are work-shy.   This is patently not the
case.   What it does mean is that among the unemployed
young people there is a proportion who openly admit that
they would rather be without work than assign themselves
to doing the kind of work they would dislike.

LEISURE

An obvious and direct consequence of unemployment is a
sudden increase in the availability of leisure time.   The
impact of unemployment upon people's leisure needs and the
changing demands placed on leisure resources has become
an important area of study in its own right.   For example,
M.A. Smith and A.F. Simpkins, working for the Centre of
Leisure Studies at the University of Salford, have recently
produced a study entitled 'Unemployment and Leisure: a
review and some proposals for research'.

One of the ironies of unemployment is that, at the very
time when the unemployed individuals have more opportunity
for leisure pursuits, their financial situation makes it more
difficult or impossible for them to indulge in leisure
activities.   This irony is compounded in a time of mass
unemployment and economic recession through the cut-backs
and reductions in the subsidies to such areas as leisure
pursuits and adult education.

The first aim of this part of the survey was to obtain an
indication of the proportion of young people who felt
dissatisfied with the current use they made of their leisure
time and to test whether their level of satisfaction is related
to their employment history.   39% of the long-term
unemployed said that they wished that they had more things
to do with their leisure time, compared with 32% both of the
short-term unemployed and of those who had no recent
experience of unemployment.   This confirms the kind of
observations made by a number of case studies of the
unemployed (for example, the work of Marsden and Duff)
that, in the initial stages of unemployment, the unemployed

discover all sorts of immediate activites to occupy their time. It is after unemployment has gone on for a while that time really begins to drag heavily and leisure is more likely to become a burden.

Not only are the long-term unemployed more likely to wish that they had more things to do to fill their leisure time, they are actually more likely to engage in less leisure activities than either the employed or the short-term unemployed. The experience of long-term unemployment so erodes their sense of purpose in life and their interest in living that they become lethargic about the way in which they spend their leisure time. Because they are more bored with their leisure time they actually undertake less leisure activities. The long-term unemployed are less likely to spend time reading books, looking at the newspaper or listening to the television or radio news broadcasts than those who are in work. The overwhelming feeling of pointlessness which sometimes accompanies long-term unemployment erodes their interest in what is going on around them and saps their motivation.

Another indication of this same phenomenon is the way in which the unemployed feel that they take a lower interest in sport than those who are in work. 77% of the members of the Centymca Club who had no recent history of unemployment said that they take an active interest in sport. This proportion drops to 70% of the short-term unemployed and 67% of the long-term unemployed. 58% of the members of the Centymca Club who had no recent experience of unemployment said that they often watch sport in their leisure time. This proportion drops to 39% of the short-term unemployed and 44% of the long-term unemployed.

In part, this lower level of participation and interest in sport may be explained as cost related. Certainly it is an expensive pastime to engage in some sports and to pay to watch them. On the other hand, this argument does not account for the lower interest in the sports coverage of television or radio, and can therefore be seen as an indication of the lethargy that seems to accompany the experience of unemployment.

The second aim of this section is to examine the response of the young people to the range of leisure facilities and activities afforded within the Centymca Club itself. There are two purposes behind this analysis: to provide an understanding of the kind of activities these young people wish to engage in during their leisure time, and to explore whether there are any marked differences between the leisure preferences of the employed and the unemployed young people. Within the Centymca Club there are fifty-two main leisure facilities and activities from which the young members can select. These fifty-two options were listed in the Centymca Attitude Inventory and the young members were asked to indicate in which of them they were likely to take an interest.

The first piece of information to emerge from an analysis of the replies to this section of the Centymca Attitude Inventory is that the young people who had experienced unemployment were likely to indicate an interest in a slightly wider range of activities and facilities than those who had not had this experience. This difference is particularly interesting in light of the observation made earlier in this chapter, namely that the young unemployed tend actually to do less things with their leisure time. The point seems to be that the young unemployed, especially those who have been out of work for some time, need the challenge of fresh opportunities and fresh possibilities. Once confronted by this challenge, they seem able to envisage their ability to respond to it.

In many ways the potential leisure time interests of the young unemployed do not differ radically from the interests of their employed contemporaries. In relationship to thirty-seven of the fifty-two facilities or activities listed in the Centymca Attitude Inventory the young unemployed did not register a different level of interest from the young employed. To this extent, a leisure centre like the Centymca Club can cater equally for the needs of the employed and the unemployed without calculating differential usage levels for the two groups.

The remaining fifteen activities or facilities, which did successfully differentiate between those who had experienced unemployment and those who had not experienced unemployment, have an interesting story to relate about the different perceptions which the two groups hold of their leisure needs. Three main differences appear. First, the young unemployed felt a greater need simply to be able to meet people and to make friends. In a way, this is an attempt to compensate for the loss of the social relationships that can be formed and maintained through work. Consequently, the young unemployed took a greater interest in the lounge area, the coffee bar and the disco.

The second observation is one which both complements and contradicts the first. As well as wanting to place themselves in situations which are likely to foster the meeting of other people and the development of new friendship patterns, the young unemployed also tended to select recreational activities which they can fasten onto without the support of friends. Consequently, the young unemployed showed a greater interest in some of the solitary pursuits of the club, like film shows, the painting and drawing classes, the dark room and yoga classes.

While the first two differences have concentrated on the higher level of interest shown among the young unemployed, the third difference brings together the activities in which the young unemployed displayed a lower level of interest. Most of these are relatively strenuous activities like badminton, circuit training and the use of the sports hall. It seems that the unemployed were less likely to want to exert themselves physically and to wear themselves out during their leisure time activity.

Turning to the more general question regarding the relative popularity of the various leisure facilities or activities among the whole membership group, by far the most popular provision is the indoor swimming pool. This appealed to 86% of the young members. Second in popularity, after the swimming pool, comes the coffee bar which was of importance to 72% of the young members. Next in popularity come the badminton and squash courts which appealed to 52% and 50% of the young people respectively.

Between 40% and 50% of the young people indicated an interest in using the lounge area, the sauna and the solarium. Between 30% and 40% of the young people wished to use the sports hall, dance classes, keep fit, billiards, film shows, table tennis, disco and weight training facilities. Just over 20% of the young people were interested in the tennis facilities and the reading room. Between 10% and 20% of the young people claimed an interest in gymnastics, circuit training, basket ball, the photographic club, yoga classes, the dark room, trampolining classes, the subaqua club, martial arts, swimming classes and parachuting courses.

After the more popular facilities there are a number of minority interest groups which appealed to less than 10% of the young people. These include the chess club, judo, painting and drawing classes, slimnastics courses, the craft workshops, do-it-yourself classes, volley ball, the soccer club, slimming classes, the audio studio, camping expeditions, climbing, handball, rock climbing, kuk sool won classes, the exhibition facilities, the mountaineering club, the chapel, the bridge club, the cricket club, the newspaper, bible study and the Duke of Edinburgh Award Scheme. One of the great strengths of a club which is able to cater for a membership of 7,000 is the way in which a membership of this size enables such a diversity of minority interests to flourish.

10. Summary

The previous six chapters have provided a number of insights into the attitudes that go hand in hand with the experience of unemployment. By looking at the attitudinal areas discussed in those chapters, one by one, we have systematically organised a wealth of detail about the way in which these young people see life. The journey through these chapters has been rather like a conducted tour through the rich and varied experiences of the separate rooms of a museum or art gallery. We have been able to stop and pause in each room and to absorb the details of the particular material on display. Now, having come to the end of the tour, we need to be able to stand back and to reflect on what we have observed. What does it all add up to, and what does it all mean?

When a number of individuals go home from their visit to an exhibition, each one is likely to take with him or her a different impression. Different things strike home to different people, because we all come with our own particular set of experiences, interests and expectations. The same thing will happen to the material presented in the preceding chapters. Some readers will have been particularly struck by the political attitudes, the moral attitudes or the religious attitudes of the young people. Others will have paid special attention to the young person's self image, their well-being, their worries, or their counselling needs. How can a summary be made of this material? Is the author simply to rely on his subjective judgement and intuition to pick up the points that interest him most, or is there a more objective way in which he can set to work?

I decided quite clearly to reject the subjective approach. I saw no particular value in foisting my own interests, prejudices and interpretations onto the reader. I decided, instead, to look at the range of objective techniques available to summarise such a mass of detailed information; and I chose to use the statistical procedure known as 'factor analysis'. In order to understand what is achieved by factor analysis, it is necessary to recall the way in which the raw data were collected in the first place. This means looking closely at the construction of the Centymca Attitude Inventory.

At first glance the Centymca Attitude Inventory consists of 140 short sentences. People are asked to respond to these 140 sentences by indicating their level of agreement on a five point scale from 'agree strongly' and 'agree', through 'not certain', to 'disagree' and 'disagree strongly'. Because of the explicit purpose behind the design of this attitude inventory, these 140 items were intended to give information about twelve key areas: namely well-being, worry, beliefs, values, self image, counselling, morals, law, politics, society, work and leisure. What we need to do now is to explore whether there are any other meaningful ways in which these items can be organised in order to present an insightful summary of what the previous chapters have said.

Before going on to the process of factor analysis itself, the first stage in this summarizing exercise requires the use of the simpler technique, from which factor analysis is derived, known as 'correlational analysis'. This first stage means that we correlate each of the 140 items independently with the young persons' experience of unemployment. The correlation coefficent gives a measure of the extent to which two variables, or pieces of information, co-vary or fluctuate in association with each other. In the present situation, we wish to know which of the 140 items in the Centymca Attitude Inventory co-vary with the young persons' experience of unemployment. In other words, we wish to pick out those items with which the unemployed tend either to agree or to disagree more readily than the employed.

Again I used the 5% probability level to determine which items had a significant correlation with unemployment. This technique picked out fifty-three of the 140 items as being worth further consideration. These fifty-three items are listed in Appendix One, together with their correlation coefficient with unemployment, in the random sequence in which they appear in the Centymca Attitude Inventory.

In order to understand these correlation coefficients, it is necessary to look both at their size and the direction of the sign in front of them. A correlation coefficient of zero means that there is no relationship at all, while a correlation coefficient of one means that there is a perfect relationship. It follows from this that the larger correlation coefficients indicate a stronger relationship. The correlation coefficients in this appendix vary between .0405 and .1364. It must be remembered that even the smallest of these correlation coefficients indicates a stronger relationship than one which would have been likely to occur by chance at least five times in a hundred.

The positive sign preceding the correlation coefficient means that the two variables co-vary in the same direction. This is best illustrated by taking an actual example. There is a positive correlation (+.1146) between the experience of unemployment and item 54, 'I have sometimes considered taking my own life'. This means that the unemployed were more likely to agree with that statement and to say that they had sometimes considered taking their own life.

The negative sign preceding the correlation coefficient means just the opposite from this. That is to say that the negative sign shows that there is still a real relationship between the item and the experience of unemployment, but that they co-vary in the opposite direction. An example of this is the negative correlation (-.1029) between unemployment and item 1, 'I listen to the radio or television news nearly every day'. This means that the unemployed were more likely to disagree with the statement and to say that they did not listen to the radio or television news nearly every day.

Looking at the column of correlation coefficients in Appendix One, we are still left with a problem not much different from the one we faced when we first tried to summarise the conclusions of the preceding six chapters. It is true that we can now see all of the significant items at a glance, and next to them we find an indication of the direction and strength of their relationship with unemployment, but it still has not helped us to pull out the main trends underlying these separate items. So it is now that factor analysis comes into its own.

The idea of factor analysis is to take the fifty-three items, which we know all correlate with the experience of unemployment, and ask the extent to which these items intercorrelate among themselves. In other words, this is a statistical technique designed to detect whether there is a mathematical pattern underlying people's responses to the individual items. It is this pattern which is known as the factor structure of a set of items. It is the factor structure which provides us with an objective method of summarising the mass of detail which confronts us.

The type of factor analysis which I used is known as a 'Principal Factor Solution, Unrotated'. The function of this type of factor analysis is to look for the strongest pattern of relationships among the items and to identify this first as the principal factor. The technique then looks for the next strongest pattern of relationships and identifies this as the second factor. The process continues, with each next factor being weaker than the one before, until finally the process stops.

Appendix Two sets out the results of factor analysis applied to all the fifty-three items. Instead of computing just one factor solution, I computed three: one on the total sample of the responses of all the 1,085 young people; one on the responses just of the young people who had experienced unemployment; and one on the responses just of the young people who had not experienced unemployment. These three solutions were computed separately in order to make sure that the answer did not vary from group to group. For example, it is theoretically possible that one set of relationships could occur among the young people who had experienced unemployment, while another pattern could occur among the young people who had not experienced unemployment. In the event, as Appendix Two admirably demonstrates, all three solutions came to the same conclusion and produced the same basic patterns. This gives us much more confidence in the proposed answer.

What we learn from Appendix Two is this. Underlying those fifty-three items, there are two main factors. These can be identified by inspecting the factor loadings, which work much in the same way as correlation coefficients. The most important thing is the size of the factor loading. Then the preceding sign tells us whether the individual item is positively or negatively related to the factor on which it loads.

In describing the two factors underlying the fifty-three items I have followed the convention of selecting those items which generally have a factor loading around .30 or above. For the sake of clarity I have underlined the factor loadings which I consider contribute significantly to the two main factors. On factor one there are sixteen items, while on factor two there are fourteen items. The figures at the bottom of the table in Appendix Two, described as 'eigenvalues' and 'percentage of variance', are indicators of the respective importance of the two factors. Factor one is clearly the more important of the two.

The next step in the process is to define what these two factors mean in terms of their psychological interpretation. The first factor emerges as a dimension measuring depression. Those who had recent experience of unemployment tended to report more symptoms of depression than those who had not had recent experience of unemployment. The second factor emerges as a dimension measuring radicalism versus conservatism. The young people who had recent experience of unemployment tended to be more radical in their attitudes than those who had not had this experience. The two major attitudinal correlates of unemployment among young people emerge, therefore, as depression and radicalism.

Before examining in greater detail the psychological significance of these two factors, it is necessary to explore a little more deeply their psychometric properties. The first matter to explore is how satisfactorily the sixteen items, identified by factor one, cohere to form a scale which measures depression, and how satisfactorily the fourteen items, identified by factor two, cohere to form a scale that measures radicalism. What the research psychologist wants to know about in this case is a statistic known as the 'alpha coefficient'. The sixteen items of the depression scale produce an alpha coefficient of .8523. This is a very satisfactory index of internal consistency or reliability. The fourteen items of the radicalism scale produce an alpha coefficient of .7144. While lower than the alpha coefficient produced by the depression scale, this is still a satisfactory index of internal consistency and reliability. This means that it is legitimate for us to proceed to talk about these two factors as a scale of depression and as a scale of radicalism.

It is now possible to compute depression scores and radicalism scores for each of the 1,085 young people in our sample. Their depression score was computed by adding together their scores on each of the sixteen items that form the depression scale. Their radicalism score was computed by adding together their scores on each of the fourteen items that constitute the radicalism scale.

The other piece of information which it is important to look at is the nature of the correlation that exists between the scores on the radicalism scale and the scores on the depression scale, and also the correlations that exist between depression and unemployment and between radicalism and unemployment. To begin with there is a correlation of +.1084 between the depression scale and the experience of unemployment. This gives further confirmation to the fact that young people who had recent experience of unemployment tended to be more depressed than those who had not had this experience. Second, there is a correlation of -.1074 between the radicalism scale and unemployment. In the case of the radicalism scale, the lower the scale score, the greater is the degree of radicalism. Thus this correlation coefficient also confirms the fact that the young people who had recent experience of unemployment were more radical in their outlook than those who had not had this experience. Finally, there is a correlation of +.0870 between scores on the depression scale and scores on the radicalism scale. All of these correlation coefficients are significant beyond the 0.1% level of probability.

The really fascinating fact to emerge from these correlation coefficients is that there is a positive correlation between the depression scale and the radicalism scale. This means that we would naturally expect depressed people to be more conservative in their outlook rather than more radical. Now in the case of the psychological correlates of unemployment, we expect young people who have been unemployed to be both more depressed and more radical. This is a further piece of evidence to suggest that the tendency towards both depression and radicalism are two independent factors associated with the experience of unemployment, rather than one of these factors being a primary cause which leads on naturally to the other.

The next step in the process is to define what these two factors of depression and radicalism actually mean in terms of their psychological interpretations. The depression factor brings together notions of loneliness, anxiety, worry, isolation, self doubt, despondency and dependency. The young people who were depressed tended to say that they often feel lonely and that they feel that no-one really knows them. They were the people who worry a lot about what they are doing. They were unhappy in their work and ill at ease among those they work with. They were easily discontented with their employment and frequently feel that they ought to be looking for something else to do.

Depression erodes their ability to get on with other people. They become very anxious about their relationships with others and they worry a lot about their sex lives. They begin to doubt their worth as individuals and despair about their ability to cope with life. They tended to to be anxious about the risks of having a breakdown. They felt that they are cut off from other people and that they live isolated lives. They longed for other people to shake their despondency and to lift them out of their depression. They longed to become dependent and to turn to others for affection and for advice.

More explicitly, the young people who score highly on the depression scale openly admitted to the fact they they often feel depressed and that they do not find their lives really worth living. These were the young people who sometimes feel so bad about things that they consider taking their own life.

The radicalism syndrome is best understood as the opposite end to the conservative approach to life. Radicalism rejects the traditional values and outlooks of society which conservatism fights to maintain. Radicalism brings together the rejection of conservative moral, social, economic, religious and political values.

The radical young person wants to reject the moral values that society imposed on issues like abortion, divorce, homosexuality and the use of drugs. They rejected the demands placed on them by the law of the land. They have grown to resent the imposition of rules and regulations and they have learned to distrust and dislike the police. Their interest is in enjoying the present moment, not in saving up for their future. Politically, they reject all that the Conservative party stands for. Their support is on the side of the trade unions. They have little time for religious beliefs. They reject God and all that the church stands for. They have little time for the clergy and wish to see religious education removed from schools.

By way of summary, what this chapter serves to do is to demonstrate that there are two main psychological correlates of unemployment among young people. These two factors have been characterised as depression and radicalism. As more and more young people experience the psychological costs of unemployment, so society must be more prepared to accept the consequences of young people being increasingly depressed with their lives and increasingly radical in their rejection of the society which they feel has in its own turn rejected them.

Character Sketches

The purpose of the previous chapters has been to make generalisations and predictions about the ways in which the attitudes of the sixteen to twenty-five year olds who have experienced unemployment differ from those who have not had that experience. Some important trends have emerged, especially in the identification of the two factors of depression and radicalism. At the same time, it needs to be stressed that there is a great deal of variation and many differences among the young unemployed themselves.

Chapter 3 demonstrated that, in the 1980s, unemployment has come to affect the lives of young people from all walks of life. The detailed attitudes of the young unemployed are as diverse as the different backgrounds from which they have come. For this reason, I am anxious that the generalisations presented in the previous chapters should be balanced by the opportunity to meet the distinctiveness and individuality of some of the young people who might otherwise be hidden beneath the generalisations.

As well as leading to generalisations, the information collected by the Centymca Attitude Inventory also enables us to draw up detailed character sketches for each of the individuals who co-operated in the project. Space does not permit a large number of detailed character studies, but a few such studies can usefully serve to illustrate the richness of the data and remind us that, beneath the statistical generalisations, we are dealing with uniqueness and individuality the whole time. In the last analysis, one of the greatest benefits of sociological generalisations about young people is the way in which these generalisations help us to gain insight into the individuals whom we know and among whom we work.

The character studies presented in this section are not claimed to be representative of the young unemployed in any sense. There is possibly no such thing as a typical unemployed young person. The few people presented for in-depth study were chosen virtually at random from the group of young people who had experienced at least twelve months unemployment during the past two years.

LIVINGSTONE

Livingstone is a twenty year old West Indian youth. Both of his parents were born in Jamaica, but they had moved to London just before his own birth. Livingstone has grown up in London and therefore regards himself as a Londoner. He is single and still lives at home with his parents, about seven miles from the city centre. Livingstone left school at the earliest opportunity at the age of sixteen with a few CSEs, but no O levels. Since leaving school he has discovered that work is difficult to find. Not long before joining London Central YMCA, he managed to obtain a job as a packer working for a clothing manufacturer. He describes his job as 'packing evening dresses and sending them out to shops all over the country'. Before finding his present job, Livingstone had spent more that eighteen months of the previous two years unemployed.

Finding work at last seems to have done Livingstone a lot of good. He says that he now finds his life really worth living and that he feels that he has a sense of purpose in life. Basically Livingstone is a happy, outgoing sort of person. He likes to have a lot of people around him and he is very much at home in crowds. He does not think of himself as the kind of person who often feels depressed or ever becomes suicidal. He has quite a lot of confidence in his worth as a person and in his ability to cope with life as it comes.

Livingstone has no shortage of friends. He is rarely lonely since he feels that he is able to draw on people who know him well for affection and for advice when he needs it. Although he has lived in London all his life, Livingstone is far from certain that he is really at home in England or that he actually likes living here. In fact, he says that he often thinks of moving away from England to find better prospects elsewhere.

His happy, outgoing nature means that Livingstone does not often suffer from personal doubts or worries. He does not worry much about his physical health or about his mental welfare. Livingstone does not find relationships a source of worry either. The personal matter which does worry him, however, is the thought of growing older. Livingstone's experience of life so far, in being a non-achiever at school, in experiencing long periods of unemployment and in earning so little as a packer, have not given him a great deal of confidence in the future. Looking beyond the present to the time when he will want a home and family of his own begins to fill Livingstone with anxiety.

In spite of giving the appearance of being relatively happy-go-lucky in his attitude to life, Livingstone takes quite a responsible attitude to things that really matter. He takes his work seriously and often worries about it. He also worries about financial matters and is concerned about running up debts.

From time to time Livingstone feels the need to talk his problems over with someone. His family have always been a great support to him when he has wanted to talk. He says that he has found it very helpful to talk about his problems with his father and his mother. He has also been helped by talking with close friends, but to a lesser extent than by talking to his parents. In the past he has never turned to professional people for help. Looking to the future, should the need and opportunity arise, Livingstone says that he would be willing to turn to a minister of religion for advice, but never to a trained counsellor.

Having been unemployed for so long, Livingstone gives quite a high priority to money. He says that it is important to him to be earning money and, having earned it, he attaches importance to being able both to save for the future and to spend in the present. On the one hand, he feels that it will be important for him to own his own house some day. On the other hand, he feels that having a good time now is very important also.

Personal values take a high priority in Livingstone's life. He takes trouble over his appearance and it matters to him a great deal what other people think about him. Family and friends are very important in making his life worth living. Social values are much less important to Livingstone. Politics plays no part in his life at all, and he is not sure whether religion or moral values rate at all highly with him.

Livingstone is basically honest and likeable, but he is not very bright and rarely practices introspection or self analysis. He wants to project a good public image of himself and generally believes that image to be true. He wants to think of himself as the kind of person who never breaks his promise or tells lies. He says that he has never stolen anything in his life and that he is always willing to admit when he makes a mistake. He considers that he has never taken advantage of people or felt resentment when he failed to get his own way.

In spite of his protestation about personal honesty and integrity, Livingstone holds the law itself in low regard; he does not mind admitting that he tries to dodge the law when he thinks that he can get away with it. For example, he sees nothing wrong in travelling without a ticket or evading the customs if you are not caught. Livingstone does not reckon that either of these are serious offences and he considers that he is quick witted enough to get away with them. On the other hand, he is more overawed by the officialdom of the income tax system and he feels that it is wise to complete tax returns with complete honesty. As a motorist also, Livingstone is inclined to try to get away with motoring offences. Speed limits and parking rules are both tiresome restrictions which can be ignored. More significantly, Livingstone does not consider it wrong to drink and drive if you can get away with it.

Religion plays no part in Livingstone's life at all. He is not a practising member of any religious group. He says that he has never attended a church service in his life, and that it is now more than five years since he last prayed or read the bible, and then this was at school. Indeed, Livingstone does not believe that there is anything beyond this life, since he rejects all belief in life after death. In spite of his lack of involvement with religion, Livingstone is in no sense antagonistic towards the church. He does not feel that the church and the bible are irrelevant for life today, but simply that he has no direct contact with them. Moreover, he does not wish to remove religious education from its place in schools. In fact, Livingstone says that he believes in God and in Jesus Christ, although he has in no sense worked out the implications of such beliefs for his own life.

On matters of morality, Livingstone adopts a liberal view towards sexual ethics, but a conservative view towards drugs. He strongly rejects the notion that there is anything wrong in having sexual intercourse outside marriage or in an unmarried couple living together. He equally strongly rejects the notion that there is anything wrong in homosexual relationships. On the other hand,

Livingstone comes out strongly against the use of heroin and marijuana, while keeping an open mind on the abuse of alcohol. Contraception presents no moral difficulties for Livingstone at all: he has grown up in a world where this is totally acceptable. On the other hand, Livingstone does not accept abortion as morally right and he does not know what to think about euthanasia.

Like religion, politics is of no practical importance in Livingstone's life. He takes no active part in politics, and considers that it makes absolutely no difference which political party is in power. He says that he has no confidence at all in the policies of the Labour party or of the Conservative party, while he thinks that the Liberal party is the most promising of the three.

Generally, Livingstone does not hold strong views about political issues, except in the case of immigration. He declares himself strongly against any restrictions on immigration into Britain since, after all, his own family are recent immigrants to Britain themselves. He has no views one way or the other on the Common Market, on the economic influence of multi-national corporations, on the desirability of supporting home industry or on the advantages of the nationalisation of industry. On the other hand, he has made up his mind on issues like the trade unions, private schools and private medicine, although he does not feel particularly strongly about his views on these matters. Here his attitude tends to be right wing. He feels that the trade unions have too much power and that it would be wrong to abolish independent schools and private medical practice.

Livingstone's disillusionment with British society goes quite deep. He sees no real future for Britain, and his basic attitude towards his environment is one of pessimism. He feels that he is living is a decaying society, in which the crime rate is rising, the health service deteriorating and the standard of schools declining. He feels that the credit card is encouraging careless spending, that it is becoming too easy to obtain an abortion, and that pornography is too readily available. On the other hand, he does not consider that divorce is becoming too easy or that too much violence is shown on television.

When asked to assess the importance of various problems confronting today's world, Livingstone rates the most important to be the risk of nuclear war. He is very concerned about the threat of nuclear war. He says that he is also concerned about the risk of pollution to the environment, the poverty of the Third World and the people who are homeless. On the other hand, he says that he is not concerned about the consequences of inflation or about the problems of unemployment. Although he has experienced a great deal of unemployment himself, Livingstone does not consider that unemployment is an issue about which it is worth getting too worried. He feels that unemployment is a problem which today's society simply has to learn to live with.

Being back to work is very important to Livingstone. Although he worries about his work, he is basically happy in his new job as a packer. He likes the people he works with and, at the moment, he has no intention of looking around for something else. Livingstone says that he considers it important to work hard and that he wants to do well at work. He feels that he is getting much more out of having a job than merely his take home pay at the end of the week. He does not work just for the money. In fact, he says that he would rather have a job he disliked than go on social security.

Livingstone feels that he makes good use of his leisure time, and he is certainly not bored. He listens to music, reads the newspaper and watches some television nearly every day. Sport plays an important part in his leisure time activities, both as a spectator and as a participant.

Livingstone joined London Central YMCA partly because of the sports facilities, but also partly because of the social facilities. Looking through the range of facilities and activities available within London Central YMCA, he indicates that he is likely to take an interest in eighteen of the fifty-two options listed in the questionnaire: these are badminton, basket ball, billiards, circuit training, coffee bar, dance classes, the disco, film shows, gymnastics, keep fit, kuk sool won classes, martial arts, the soccer club, the sports hall, the squash courts, the swimming pool, table tennis and weight training. He feels that such a range of facilities and activities will not only lead to full and satisfying recreation, but also help him to meet people and to make new friends – something which he very much needs after his long period of unemployment.

MANDY

Mandy is a twenty year old English girl. Both her parents were born in England and she has never lived elsewhere. She was brought up in a small village in Essex, where she lived until making her way to London after leaving school at the age of sixteen without any academic qualifications. Like a number of young people who come to London to seek work, Mandy has discovered that the employment situation for unqualified young people is difficult. Currently she is doing temporary work in catering, a job which she found through an employment agency. Before finding her present job, Mandy spent half of the previous two years out of work. In London, she lives with her fiance in a house about seven miles from the city centre, which they share with Mandy's sister, her sister's boy-friend and their young child.

Mandy is a person of moods. She does not often feel depressed, but when she does the depression goes deeply and it is not unknown for her to feel so depressed that she considers taking her own life. In these moods she knows that she cannot cope and that she has ceased to value herself as a person. Then she longs for someone to turn to for advice, and even more someone to turn to for affection. In the past she has never found either of her parents really approachable or helpful when she has wanted to talk, but she has gained much more help from talking with close friends. At one point in the past Mandy turned to a trained counsellor for help and benefitted considerably from this experience. She says that she would not be hesitant to turn to a trained counsellor for professional help again should the need arise.

The influence of her background in the small Essex village means that Mandy is not properly at home with her new inner city way of life. She does not like having a lot of people around her; indeed, from time to time she feels the crowds are quite oppressive. Although she never experiences complete isolation in the city, she does tend to feel lonely, and that in spite of living with people whom she feels know her reasonably well.

The two things which seem to worry Mandy most are work and money. She is very worried about her debts, especially against her recent experience of prolonged unemployment and the temporary nature of her present job. She also has a great sense of anxiety about the uncertainty of the world situation in which she lives. By way of contrast she says that her personal life is not at present a particular source of worry for her. Her relationships are stable and her sex life is good.

Mandy does not take a great deal of personal interest in her own appearance, although she is concerned about what people think of her. She is the kind of person who gives a very high priority to her home and family; she relies quite heavily on their support, as well as on the support of her friends. Thinking about her social values, Mandy says that she has more time for religion than for politics, although neither plays a real part in her life.

Now that she has a job, Mandy feels that it is very important for her to be earning money. Her idea of earning money is not, however, to spend it straight away on having a good time. Spending money is quite unimportant to her, nor does she rate having a good time at all highly. What is important to her is saving towards the future and building some security for herself.

Mandy has quite a mature and honest self image. She is sufficiently reflective and self aware to recognise her own feelings, and sufficiently secure in herself to be willing and able to openly acknowledge her feelings to others, even when she runs the risk of placing herself in a socially undesirable light. In this way Mandy admits that she has told lies and broken her promise from time to time. She does not try to pretend that she has never stolen anything in her life. She admits that she sometimes experiences feelings of jealousy when she thinks that others are better off than she is, or feelings of resentment when she does not get her own way.

Although Mandy calls herself a Christian and says that religion is important to her, the church plays no part in her life at all; it is more than a year since she last attended a place of worship. What is important, she says, is that she believes God exists and that Jesus Christ is the Son of God. Her system of religious beliefs is quite content to reconcile the Christian teaching of life after death with the non-Christian doctrine of reincarnation. She firmly maintains that religious education should continue to have a place in schools.

In spite of her lack of involvement in a local church, Mandy feels that she holds a positive attitude towards the church. She feels that the church has quite a lot to offer the world today, but that she can get along quite well without it. Similarly, Mandy says that she holds a favourable attitude towards the bible, but it is more than a year since she last opened her own copy of the bible. Prayer is a different matter. Although Mandy does not regard herself as praying regularly, it is not unusual for her to turn to God for support in prayer.

In Mandy's world-view, religion and superstition seem to be quite closely aligned. In many ways Mandy is quite a superstitious person. She places a great deal of confidence in her horoscope and she belives that luck plays an important part in her life.

On moral issues, Mandy has developed a very convinced liberal position. She shows no hesitation in approving contraception, abortion, euthanasia, homosexuality and extra-marital sexual intercourse as morally acceptable. Similarly, she freely accepts the use of marijuana and alcohol. Where Mandy draws the line on the liberalisation of morals is concerned with the use of drugs like heroin.

Mandy has also developed a liberal attitude towards the law, especially on economic issues. Being unemployed for much of the time since leaving school, Mandy has never had much surplus income and consequently she has developed an attitude of gaining where she can at the cost of the system. She believes that it is acceptable to travel on public transport without a ticket if you can get away with it. She thinks it is foolish to declare all income to the Inland Revenue authorities. Looking at motoring laws, Mandy considers that parking offences are harmless enough, since she finds many parking restrictions unnecessary and tiresome. She sees more point in speed limits, but she is far from sure that she would ever really feel bound to observe them. What is important, she believes, is to act responsibly about not drinking and driving.

Politics play no part in Mandy's life at all. She says that she has no confidence in the policies of any of the major political parties and that it makes no difference which political party holds power. This lack of interest in politics is also reflected by the fact that she tends to feel strongly neither one way nor the other about most of the political issues included in the questionnaire. She has no views on international political issues like the Common Market, or multi-national corporations. She has no views on home political issues like the nationalisation of industry or the power of trade unions. She does not care whether private medicine is encouraged or abolished. On the few issues where Mandy has formulated political views, they tend to be conservative in nature. For example, she wishes to protect independent schools and to restrict immigration into Britain.

Political apathy is also seen behind Mandy's view of the society in which she lives. When asked a series of questions about the crime rate, the educational standard of schools, the state of the health service, or the future of Britain itself, all that Mandy can honestly say is that she has no views. However, she is much more aware of her personal reactions to the moral climate of Britian. In spite of her own predisposition towards a liberal morality, she generally feels that the whole movement towards moral liberalisation has gone too far. She believes that it is becoming too easy to obtain a divorce, that there is too much violence on television and that pornography is now too readily available. The moral issue that stands apart from the others in Mandy's evaluation of social trends is abortion; Mandy feels that it is still not easy enough to obtain abortions today.

Although politically apathetic, Mandy does not regard herself as unconcerned about the major problems that confront the world today. She says that she is concerned about such issues as the rate of inflation and the plight of people who are homeless. She is concerned about the risk to the world's future which comes from the dangers of pollution to the environment or nuclear war. On the other hand, Mandy does not feel in the least concerned about the problems of the Third World. This is totally outside her experience and her vision.

Her temporary job in catering is bringing very little by way of happiness to Mandy's life. She says that she is not happy in her job, and that she dislikes the people with whom she works. The whole time she wishes that she could change her present job for something else. Mandy believes that there should be a lot more to having a job than simply earning money. She believes that it is important to work hard and to have an ambition in life. Although she does not enjoy her present work, Mandy does not believe in accepting unemployment as the easy way out. She would rather be doing a job she dislikes than being unemployed all over again and living on social security.

When away from her job, Mandy is finding her leisure time quite full and rewarding. She is not longing for more things to fill her time off work. Her major recreational interest is sport; she enjoys both taking an active part in sport and watching others engage in sporting activities. She also watches television, listens to music and reads the newspapers.

Mandy's main reason for joining London Central YMCA was to use the sports facilites. In particular she is interested in the dance classes, the squash courts, the swimming pool and the trampolining classes. She says that she would also like to think about the parachuting courses. She is interested in the health facilites, like the facials and massage, the sauna, the solarium, slimnastics courses and slimming classes. At the same time, Mandy says that she would like to explore some of the non-sporting programme facilities of the YMCA, like the chess club, the craft work shop, the film shows and the painting and drawing classes, as well as the social facilities like the coffee bar and the lounge area.

In spite of the problems that she experienced in finding work, Mandy believes that she made the right decision in leaving her rural background and making for the city. She likes London and she is sure that she would advise other young people to follow in her footsteps. Although getting started in life in the inner city was not easy for her, Mandy feels that she has basically coped and that other young people are equipped to do the same.

PATRICK

Patrick represents quite a different kind of unemployment
problem among young people from the situations represented
by Livingstone and Mandy. Being twenty-five years of
age, Patrick is right at the upper end of the age group
under review. He is also at the upper end of the
educational continuum. Patrick grew up in Northern
Ireland, not far from the city of Belfast. After doing very
well at secondary school, Patrick came across to England to
read law for his first degree at London University. He
then stayed on to take a higher degree in law.

Leaving university with a higher degree, Patrick began to
seek an academic post as a university lecturer in law. With
the contraction of the higher educational system, he began
to realise just how little his academic qualifications were
really worth. After nearly two years of being unemployed,
Patrick eventually obtained a lectureship in one of the
London Polytechnics. Patrick is single and lives less than
a mile from the centre of London in accommodation which he
shares with other people of his own age group.

Since being in London, Patrick has built up around
himself a large network of friends, and this has helped him
to cope with his long period of unemployment. He says
that he never feels lonely or longs for people to turn to for
advice or affection. He feels that he has around him a
group of people who know him really well. Patrick feels at
home in the inner city environment. He likes to have a lot
of people around him and he enjoys being at the heart of a
crowd.

Generally Patrick feels that he is well able to cope with
life. He has never been a great worrier, but certain
things did begin to play on his mind while he was
unemployed, especially the problem of making ends meet.
Even now he is still in debt and that worries him a great
deal. Now that he has a job, he finds himself becoming
anxious about his work and about his relationships. In
spite of living through the frustrations and disappointments
of unemployment, Patrick says that he feels his life has a
sense of purpose and that he finds life really worth living.
Even when unemployed, he did not often tend to feel
depressed or begin to doubt his worth as a person.

From time to time Patrick feels the need to talk his

problems over with someone. He remembers that as a child
he used to find it helpful to talk with his mother, but he is
not so sure that he ever found it helpful to talk with his
father. Nowadays he finds that his close friends provide
more than an adequate resource when he needs help in
thinking something through. He has never turned to
professionals for help, and he is sure that he is not likely
to do so in the future.

A thoughtful and introspective person, Patrick has
developed considerable insight into his own motivation and
character. He is also sufficiently secure in himself to be
honest to others about his actions and feelings. He is
aware and acknowledges that he is the kind of person who
has felt resentment when he has not got his own way, or
jealousy when he has felt that others were better off than
himself. Sometimes Patrick has taken advantage of other
people. He does not hesitate to admit that he has told lies,
broken his promises and taken things that did not belong to
him.

Economic values have a very high priority in Patrick's
life. He argues that making money, saving money and
spending money are all very important to him. He is
looking forward to the day when he can say that he owns
his own house, but at the same time his economic
investment is in the present and in today's pleasures as
well. Personal values are also very important to Patrick.
He attaches a great deal of importance to his appearance
and he places considerable store on what people think of
him. Both his family and his friends play an important
part in his life.

Patrick is an atheist who has no time for the church or
for religion in any form. He has completely dismissed all
ideas of belief in God and believes that it is nonsense to
claim that Jesus Christ is the Son of God. As a
thorough-going secularist, Patrick believes that life beings
and ends with our present experience. He argues that
both the church and the bible are totally irrelevant for life
today, and that religious education should be removed from
the school curriculum. It is now more than five years since
Patrick last attended a place of worship or prayed,
although he reports that he has read from the bible during
the past year.

On moral questions, Patrick has developed a consistent

and thoroughly liberal attitude. He is emphatically dismissive of moral absolutes prohibiting various forms of sexual relationships, condemning the use of drugs and alcohol, or maintaining the inviolable sanctity of life. Thus, he disagrees strongly that there is anything wrong in homosexual relationships or heterosexual relationships outside marriage. He has no doubt at all about accepting both abortion and euthanasia as morally acceptable practices. He also strongly supports the right of the individual to use marijuana or to become inebriated on alcohol. To be consistent with his denial of moral absolutes Patrick also supports the right of the individual to use heroin, but he is less convinced about the acceptability of the social implications of this decision.

Looking at the moral trends of the society around him, Patrick feels that not enough progress is being made in the direction of throwing off traditional inhibitions and prohibitions. For example, he believes that society still makes it far too difficult to obtain an abortion or to secure a divorce. Similarly, he feels that there are still too many restrictions on pornography and too much censorship on television.

Patrick's moral liberalism also extends to a liberal attitude towards the law. He believes that the individual is entitled to try to get away with travelling on public transport without a ticket, with bringing an extra bottle of spirits through the customs, or with fiddling tax returns. These views give an interesting insight into the personal attitudes towards the law of a polytechnic lecturer in law. Similarly, Patrick sees no reason why the law should be upheld on the point of refusing the sale of cigarettes to children. As a motorist, Patrick sees nothing compelling in either parking restrictions or speed limits, but he does agree that the law is right in prohibiting drinking and driving.

Politically Patrick holds strongly and militantly to left-wing views. He says that his political values are important to him and that he personally takes an active part in politics, since he believes that it makes an enormous difference to the country which kind of political party holds power. Patrick's left-wing persuasions mean that he supports the nationalisation of industry and the power of the trade unions. He supports the abolition of private medicine and the outlawing of independent schools. He is strongly against any restrictions being imposed on immigration into Britain. On the international front, Patrick believes that the Common Market is a bad thing. As a consequence of his political views, Patrick does not feel able to place his confidence in any of the major British political parties. He finds the Conservative party and the Liberal party plainly inappropriate organisations for his support, and he is equally disappointed by the policies and achievements of the British Labour party.

Patrick's economic and social evaluations of different sectors of British society find him giving unqualified support to the pay claims of miners, car workers and nurses. He is strongly committed to the notion that these three groups of workers are underpaid for the job they do in society. He is less sure about doctors, although on balance he considers that they are worth more than the value currently ascribed to them in British society. Policemen and clergy are two groups which Patrick places in a completely different category. He feels that they are already too highly paid in relationship to the contribution which they make to society.

Looking at the direction in which society is moving, Patrick holds mixed views. On the one hand, he is confident in the course taken by education: he feels that the educational standard of schools is getting better, not worse. On the other hand, he feels that the standard of the health service is deteriorating and that the crime rate is rising the whole time. However, on balance, Patrick remains nothing but confident in Britian's future.

Generally Patrick shares a high level of concern about most of the problems that worry today's world. He regards himself as supporting both the environmentalist lobby and the anti-nuclear groups, since he considers that both pollution to the environment and nuclear war present very real and devastating threats to civilisation as we know it today. Patrick says that he is also concerned about the poverty of the Third World.

Patrick finds that his work is important to him and he is basically happy with his new post in the law department at the polytechnic. He likes his subject and he appreciates the opportunity to teach it, although he is not finding it easy to establish good working relationships with his colleages. He feels that there is much less corporate

identity and social life among the polytechnic staff than he
would really like. He says that he does not like the
attitude of the people with whom he finds himself working.
Having accepted this post, Patrick feels that he wants to
make the most of it. At the moment he says that he is
planning to stay there and that he has no immediate
intention of applying for posts elsewhere. He believes that
job satisfaction is very important. He does not feel that it
is worth working just for the money; he says that he would
rather go on social security than have a job he did not like
doing. Probably this is one of the reasons why he was
willing to remain unemployed for so long while waiting for
something like his present post to turn up.

Away from the polytechnic, Patrick says that he finds his
leisure time rewarding. He often reads books and listens to
music. He spends even more time watching television. He
takes an active interest in world affairs through the
newspapers and through the radio and television. When not
at home, he is often to be found drinking with friends or
taking an active part in sport. He joined London Central
YMCA because he wanted to use the sport facilities and
because he wanted to meet new people and make new
friends.

In spite of his difficulties in finding a job, Patrick is
sure that he made the right choice in leaving Northern
Ireland for London, and in staying on in London after he
had finished at London University. He likes living in
London very much and he believes that London has so much
more to offer young people than other cities. Patrick has
no time for those people who complain that London places
too many risks and dangers in the young person's path.
Reflecting back on his own six or seven years in the city,
Patrick says that he would happily advise other young
students from Northern Ireland to follow in his footsteps
and to make a home for themselves in London.

VALERIE

Valerie is another young person who discovered that, in the 1980s, a degree is no certain passport to employment. After graduating at the age of twenty-two, Valerie spent two long years seeking a suitable appointment in her home county of Lancashire. In desparation, she came South only a year ago and moved in to live with her boy friend, some ten miles or so from the centre of London. In London she was much more successful in her quest for work. Here she managed to land for herself an interesting and quite lucrative post with a firm of insurance brokers.

Finding a job after being unemployed for so long brought about a great change in Valerie's life. She says that she likes the work very much and that she is working with a pleasant group of people. She has made up her mind that she wants to stay with that firm for some time and work her way up into a position of greater responsibility. She is finding it quite a relief no longer to be on the look-out for situations vacant and no longer to be applying for jobs, always wondering whether she would be short-listed and called for interview, and then anxiously awaiting the decision of the interviewers.

Valerie is quite firm that she would be willing to do anything rather than be unemployed for so long again. She knows that she is lucky to have found at last a job which she really enjoys doing, and she emphasises the fact that, if the choice was between being unemployed again and doing a job she did not enjoy, she would chose the job every time, however much she might detest it. The contrast between being unemployed and employed in her present job has taught Valerie that there is much more to be derived from having a job than merely the cheque at the end of the month. It opens up a whole new range of interests and friendships.

Valerie spends a lot of her leisure time out and about with her friends. She says that her friends are very important to her. She spends several evenings a week in her local public house, drinking and talking with her friends. On the other evenings, she is likely to be out somewhere else, either playing sport with friends, or watching sport in their company. By way of contrast, Valerie spends very little time at home. She says that she had enough of being at home when she was unemployed, with nothing to do all day. Now she can afford to go out, she is determined to make the most of it. Her reason for joining the London Central YMCA was not that Valerie was bored with her leisure time and was looking around for more things to do, but because it was very close to her place of work and she saw it as providing an ideal opportunity for extending her interests and activities in sport.

Valerie has lived in England all her life, and both of her parents were born in England as well. She says that she likes living in England herself, and that she has never seriously thought of moving away to make a new start for herself abroad somewhere, even when she was finding' it so difficult to obtain a suitable job. Although Valerie has no desire to leave her native country, she is also far from optimistic about the prospects which England holds out to its inhabitants. She reckons that the crime rate is rising, while the educational system and the welfare state are going into decline. In fact, she is not confident at all about the kind of future that is in store for England.

Far from stimulating her into political activism, Valerie's pessimistic view of British society is accompanied by a deep seated political apathy. She says that she has no confidence in the policies of any of the three major political parties. Not only is she unwilling to commit herself to any of the major political parties, she is also unwilling to commit herself to fixed views on a number of political issues. She reckons that the problems are too complex and that she has neither the energy nor the interest to formulate her own views on them. Thus, Valerie is unwilling to commit herself one way or another on issues like the nationalisation of industry, the trade unions or immigration policy. Similarly, she is not too keen to commit herself on issues like the abolition of private medicine or the suppression of independent schools.

Looking towards the wider problems that confront today's world, Valerie shows a considerably greater degree of concern. She expresses concern for the plight of homeless refugees and for the poverty of the Third World. Nearer to home, she expresses concern about the economic situation brought about by inflation, and about the problems associated with unemployment. She also says that she takes very seriously the threats to the world's future posed by pollution and by the build-up of nuclear arms.

At the bottom of her list of values, alongside the lower position ascribed to politics, Valerie also places religion. She says that she believes in God, and she thinks that religious education should be taught in schools, but beyond this religion plays no practical part in her life. Apart from this very basic belief in the existence of God, Valerie is agnostic about most of the claims made by the church. She says that she has not firmly closed her mind against belief in Jesus Christ as the Son of God, but really she finds it hard to accept. Similarly, she has not fully closed her mind against belief in life after death, or, for that matter, belief in reincarnation, yet again these are not beliefs that seem important to her. She cannot see what difference such beliefs would really make to her life. Valerie does not belong to a church of any sort, and it is now more than five years since she last attended a place of worship or prayed.

On questions of morality, Valerie has formulated decisively liberal views. She reckons that, as an institution, marriage is clearly out of date. She has decided to set up home with her boy friend, and she says that those who criticise an unmarried couple living together are hopelessly old fashioned. She is also quite firm that criticisms of contraception and extra-marital sexual intercourse are irrelevant taboos. She reckons that abortions should be available on demand for those who want them, and that today's society still makes abortions far too difficult to obtain. Similarly, she reckons that divorce procedures should be simplified, and again she criticises the way in which today's society still seems to make it too difficult to get divorced.

The liberal nature of her views on marriage and family life is also consistently carried over into other areas of sexuality. She reckons that society should be much more open to the acceptance of homosexuality, since she believes that homosexual relationships can be as stable and as satisfactory as heterosexual relationships. She also reckons that far too much fuss is made about the availability of pornography and the screening of sex and violence on television. She feels that censorship is bad and that people should be free to choose for themselves what they want to see, and to make up their own minds about what is to influence their lives.

Alcohol is another area in which Valerie has adopted a very tolerant attitude. She says that she can see no harm in people becoming drunk, provided that they do not make a nuisance of themselves or endanger themselves or others. She would never condone drinking and driving, but drinking by itself is quite a different matter. Valerie takes a stricter line in relationship to drugs than she adopts in relationship to alcohol. She does not believe that it is wrong to use marijuana, but neither is she willing to give it her whole-hearted support in the same way that she supports the use of alcohol. She is much more doubtful still about heroin.

Her liberal views on morality stem from a deep seated conviction about the need to protect the freedom of the individual against the inhibitions of traditional mores, rather than a rebellion against the sanctions imposed by society. Thus, when it comes to an analysis of her response to the law of the land, Valerie emerges as a very law-abiding citizen. She has no desire to fight against the rules and regulations established by the legal system. She says that she thinks that speed limits and parking restrictions should be strictly obeyed; that rules about selling cigarettes to children should be carefully observed, and that tax returns should be filled in with scrupulous accuracy. She would never condone trying to travel on public transport without a ticket. Her obedience to the law is not, however, too good to be true. Valerie insists that she would be willing to bring an extra bottle of spirits though the customs without declaring it.

Valerie is a very honest and open person about her own feelings and actions. She says that she always tries to admit when she makes a mistake, and she hopes that other people will treat her in the same way. She openly admits to sometimes being jealous of other people when they seem to be getting more out of life than she is. She openly admits to sometimes feeling very resentful of other people when they stand in her path and prevent her from getting her own way. She knows that she has sometimes broken her promises and told lies. She openly confesses that she has sometimes taken advantage of people. On the other hand, Valerie reckons that she has /always been scrupulously honest in the sense that she has never taken anything that did not belong to her.

Friends are very important to Valerie and she derives a lot of support from them. She never feels really lonely, although quite often she feels in need of more personal affection than she receives. Depression is something from which Valerie has never suffered. She cannot remember ever doubting her own self worth, even when she was unemployed for so long. She has never worried about her ability to cope with life or found life intolerable. On the whole she says that she finds her life really worth living and that her life has a real sense of purpose.

Valerie allows very few things to really worry her. She takes her work seriously, but she does not worry about it. She finds money important and she experienced a lot of financial difficulties while she was unemployed, but she does not reckon that she ever really worries about her debts. Her friendships and relationships are also important to her, but again she never lets them worry her. She feels fit in herself and does not give a lot of worry to her health. However, looking to the future, she says that she does sometimes begin to worry about growing old and ill.

Generally, Valerie is very well able to cope with life as it comes, but occasionally she finds that she really needs to talk her problems over with someone. When she was a child, she used to turn to her mother, but never felt that her father was of any real help to her. Nowadays, she turns to close friends. Valerie has never had any experience of going to counsellors or clergymen for professional help, and she says that she would be extremely reluctant to turn to them in the future. She reckons that she ought to be able to stand on her own feet and that to turn to professionals for help would be an extreme sign of weakness. Valerie is most unlikely, therefore, ever to turn to the counselling facilities provided by London Central YMCA while she is in membership there.

Valerie's positive approach to life seems to have equipped her to live through her long period of unemployment without making her bitter and without destroying her independent spirit.

DAVE

Dave is an eighteen year old youth who was born in
Manchester. He left his inner city secondary school at the
earliest possible opportunity at the age of sixteen. The
bleak employment situation in Manchester for school leavers
was one of the primary factors which encouraged Dave to
move right away from home and to head for London. He
has now been living in London for nearly two years.
Currently he is sharing a house, with a number of other
young people roughly his own age, at about seven miles
distance from the city centre. He is single and has no
permanent or stable relationships.

Coming to London without a job to go to, Dave had little
real idea how difficult it would be to become established
there and to find appropriate and worthwhile employment.
Looking back now over the past two years, he is still
inclined to think that his move to London was all a
mistake. He is firmly convinced that if other young people
were ever to ask his advice before setting out to follow in
his footsteps, he would advise them strongly against doing
so.

Dave spent the whole of his first year in London being
unemployed and looking for a job. He says that during
this period he often felt that he wanted to be able to turn
to someone for understanding and advice. He felt that
back home his father would certainly have been of no help
to him, and probably his mother would have been of no
help either. Dave had never had the sort of relationships
with his parents which had enabled him to talk with them
and to expect them to be helpful and understanding. Down
in London, Dave took the only route open to him and talked
endlessly with the other young people around him. Dave
had never been used to turning to professional people for
help and so it never even occurred to him when he was
alone and without work in a strange city to look for any
more help or advice than he could get from the local Job
Centre.

After being unemployed for a year or so, Dave found
himself a back-room job in a London casino. Dave is far
from happy with this job. He finds the hours long and
anti-social, and he does not feel it is worthwhile for the low
wages that he is being paid. He reckons that he made a

mistake taking this job in the first place, and that he was better off unemployed, when he was drawing unemployment benefit. He says that what makes it worse is that he has no time for the people he has to work with, and the job itself seems so pointless.

Dave feels that time has really dragged heavily since leaving school, because there is so little that is interesting to do every day. Dave feels that, if had been unemployed any longer, he would have gone out of his mind with boredom. He would watch television, listen to music and walk about the streets; and that was about it. He had never been the sort of person to like being at home all day long. He has no interest in reading and things like that. Dave says that he really longed for a good social life. Friends are important to him, and he liked the idea of being able to go out for a drink, but he was hardly ever able to afford to do so when he was out of a job. Sport is important to him as well and he liked the idea of having a lot of free time both to take part in sport and to watch sport, but again he was hardly ever able to afford to take a true interest in such things when he was out of a job. Now that he has got a job, Dave feels that money is a little less tight, but he still needs to be very careful about the way he spends it.

In spite of the high membership fees, Dave feels that his subscription to the London Central YMCA was a very good use of the limited money that he had available to spend on his leisure time activities. He says that he joined the club both because he wanted to use the excellent sports facilities and because he thought that the social facilities would help him as well. He wanted somewhere to be able to go and to enjoy himself when he was not at work. London Central YMCA seems to have been the ideal solution to Dave's needs. In particular, he says that he wants to make use of the swimming pool and the sports hall, the sauna and the solarium. He reckons that he spends quite a lot of time in the coffee bar and the lounge area. He also takes an interest in handball, yoga classes and the martial arts.

The long period of unemployment and the unsatisfactory nature of his present job are both casting a long shadow over Dave's attitude to life. He says that, as things are, he completely lacks a sense of purpose and direction in his life. He lacks a sense of identity and self worth. In short, life is not worth living. Dave often goes through periods of real depression and not infrequently ends up feeling dangerously suicidal. When he comes to the end of his tether, he really begins to doubt his ability to cope and questions the whole point of going on.

Dave feels that one of the worst things about being unemployed is the complete feeling of isolation and loneliness that can begin to take over your life. At times, since arriving in London, Dave has been acutely lonely, in spite of, or perhaps even because of, sharing a house with a number of other young people. It would not have been so bad if all the others had been unemployed as well, but the fact that they had jobs only served to sharpen Dave's feelings of isolation. Indeed, even now he is sometimes frighted of walking out into the city. Not only did he find it extremely lonely being at home, he also found the crowds in the city very oppressive as well.

That deep seated feeling of depression colours Dave's attitude towards a number of different aspects of life. Depression affects his understading of himself: he worries about his health and future. Depression affects his understanding of his relationships: he worries about the way he is getting on with other people. He becomes obsessed with what people are thinking about him and he tends to imagine the worst. He worries about his sex life and his ability to relate to girls. Depression affects his attitude towards his job: he is worried that his job will get on top of him and that he will fail to cope with it. Dave has grown to distrust his own self judgement. He distrusts his ability to cope with his emotions and to predict the way he is going to feel about things.

Underneath it all, Dave has grown to experience quite a deep seated resentment against the society which he blames for his present situation. This resentment is seen most clearly in his attitude towards the police and the law. Dave does not feel that he owes any respect to the system at all, and he is out to beat the system where he can. When he is short of money and needs to travel into work, he tries to get away without paying his fare.

Moral questions are not issues to which Dave has ever given much thought, and he certainly does not regard moral values as of great importance in his life. He seems to have come from a morally conservative background. While largely trying to break away from this background, he has not thoroughly overthrown it. For example, he refuses to condemn the use of drugs like marijuana or the abuse of alcohol, and yet at the same time he is ill at ease in accepting these behaviours. Similarly, while he refuses to condemn sex outside marriage or the practice of homosexuality, he remains strictly conservative in his attitude towards questions like abortion, euthanasia and contraception. In particular, he is strongly convinced that euthanasia is morally wrong, while he also consistently refuses to condone any form of contraception or abortion.

Another indication of the tension in his moral standards is seen in the way in which Dave comments on the moral trends displayed in society. Since he has not yet worked out whether to support the conservative trends of his home background or the greater liberalisation of his new life style, Dave does not really know how to interpret current social trends. Sometimes he feels that society may be making it too easy to have an abortion; at other times he feels that society has not moved far enough in the direction of liberalisation. Sometimes he feels that society may be making it too easy to get divorced; at other times he feels that society has not moved far enough in the direction of the liberalisation of the divorce laws.

The kind of conservatism demonstrated by Dave's moral attitudes is also reflected in his attitude towards religion. Dave had no doubt in his mind about the existence of God or about the divinity of Jesus Chrost. He firmly believes in life after death and confidently hopes for a place in heaven when he dies. But this is where Dave's religion both begins and ends. He sees no point in belonging to a church or in reading the bible. Indeed, he has come to identify the church with the hostile society against which he is rebelling. As far as he is concerned, the church has absolutely no relevance for life today. Although he believes in God, he argues strongly against the place of religious education in schools.

Another interesting feature of Dave's world view is the way in which he has failed to make up his mind about superstitious beliefs. He no longer really believes in his horoscope, and yet he has not successfully turned his back on it. He no longer really believes that luck plays an important part in his life, and yet again he has not succeeded in rejecting the possibility. This is all part of the great confusion and uncertainty that surrounds his life.

If Dave does not show much real interest in religion, he reckons that he has even less real interest in politics. He feels that he is politically powerless and that the political decisions which really matter are all taken by other people in other places. Dave reckons that it makes no practical difference to him which political party is in power and he sees no point in voting at election time. When pressed on the point, he says that he has no confidence in the policies of any of the major political parties. He rejects them one by one. At the same time he has no real opinions on major political issues.

Dave does not appear to take much interest in the world around him. He is left unconcerned by the big political and social problems, like the pollution of the environment or the risk of nuclear war. He says that he is powerless to do anything about issues like these, so why should he worry about them? On the wider front, he says that he has no interest in issues like the poverty of the Third World or the homeless refugees. The only contemporary issues about which he does have feelings are unemployment and inflation. When world problems begin to bite into the spending power of the money in his own pocket, then Dave begins to sit up and to take notice.

Dave feels that the economic situation is making life in England worse the whole time. He feels that law and order are breaking down and he lays a lot of the blame for this at the feet of the ethnic minority groups. Dave's depression with life and his feelings of political powerlessness can lead potentially into a great deal of prejudice and hostility. In his more positive moments, Dave dreams about building a better future for himself in America. In his more negative moments, Dave could find himself at the centre of a lot of neighbourhood unrest and aggression right here in the centre or suburbs of London.

ANNA MARY

Anna Mary was born in Nigeria of Nigerian parents. She moved to England with her parents while still quite young and the whole family settled in London. Her parents' marriage broke up while she was still at school. Her father moved out and she continued to live at home with her mother. She still resents the failure of her parents' marriage. She has very little affection for her mother, but a great deal less for her father. She really feels that her father let the whole family down by going off and leaving them.

Although she enjoyed her time at school, Anna Mary never succeeded in doing at all well with her lessons. In many ways she was quite relieved when, two years ago, she was able to leave school at the age of sixteen. She left school with just a few CSEs, but no O levels.

After leaving school, Anna Mary said that she wanted a job with some glamour and life to it. She decided to try her hand at becoming a model. Her mother paid for her to attend an agency training course, and so she thought that she was well equipped to make a thriving career for herself. The evidence of the last year or so should have disillusioned her, but it has not. She has discovered that work in modelling is not easy to come by, and that she is spending much of her time idle with no regular income. She gets by because her father makes her a small but regular allowance. She does not particuarly like to talk about this, especially in light of her negative feelings about her father. Yet she has to admit that life would be a great deal harder without it.

Being unemployed and therefore at home and around the house so much of the time, Anna Mary found that she was always under her mother's feet. This all became too much for her and she was extremely relieved when she had the opportunity to move out. She now shares a flat with her boy friend, five or six miles from the city centre.

Generally speaking, Anna Mary's moral outlook is quite conservative. The fact that she has set up home with her boy friend means that she wants to argue strongly that there is nothing wrong in an unmarried couple living together or in sex outside marriage. She is sure that there is nothing morally wrong in contraception either. However, this is almost as far as her moral liberalism takes her. In fact, she feels that the moral climate of England has moved much too far in the liberal direction. She believes that it is now becoming too easy to get a divorce. She is against the idea of abortion, and again believes that it is becoming too easy to have an abortion. Anna Mary's moral conservatism also extends to a very passionate condemnation of homosexuality and an outspoken criticism of sex and violence on television. She strongly rejects the use of drugs and condemns the abuse of alcohol.

Anna Mary also holds fairly traditional religious beliefs, at least the sort of religious beliefs that do not apparently commit her to any active religious affiliation. She is adamant about her belief in God and about her acceptance of Jesus Christ as the Son of God, although she is less sure whether she really believes in life after death. She feels that the church and the bible both have an important job to do in today's world and that religious education should continue to have a place in the school curriculum. However, Anna Mary does not take an active part in church life or belong to a particular church. She has not attended a church service within the past twelve months and it was more than five years ago when she last opened the bible. Anna Mary says that she prays occasionally, but only when she really feels in need of God's help.

Politics seem to be of no interest to Anna Mary at all. She takes no active part in politics and is very sceptical about the value of the major political parties. She feels that it should make some difference which political party is in power, and yet she has no confidence in any of the major political parties actually making this difference. When pressed about her views on specific political issues, Anna Mary does not hold many firm views. On the industrial front, she has never given much thought to the pros and cons of things like the nationalisation of industry or the trade unions. On the social front, she is not really interested in the arguments involved in the controversies over private schools and private medical practice. On the international front, she feels that questions to do with the working of the Common Market or multi-national corporations are so far from her own experience that she can safely ignore them. On the other hand, coming herself from a family which has settled in England quite recently, she does feel strongly about the political question of immigration. She feels that there should be fewer restrictions on immigration into Britian.

Anna Mary's political apathy seems to come from a deep rooted sense of powerlessness, rather than from a disinterest in what is happening in the world. Anna Mary says that she does not take an interest in politics because she has no power to influence political decisions. Nevertheless, she says that she takes a great deal of interest in what is happening in world affairs. Certainly she is aware of the major issues of world concern and she professes to take these issues seriously. Thus, at home she says that she is concerned about the problems of unemployment and inflation. Overseas, she says that she is concerned about the poverty of the Third World. On the other hand, the threat of nuclear war does not concern her; she feels at present that this kind of threat is too remote to be worth worrying about.

When asked specifically about her attitude to life in England, Anna Mary is rather non-commital. She says that she does not particularly like living in England, but that she is not sure that things are really any better elsewhere. She is not confident that there is much of a future for Britian, but at the same time she is not actively contemplating moving away to make a fresh start somewhere else.

Anna Mary is also rather non-commital about her attitude to London. Basically she likes city life; she likes to have a lot of people around her. Certainly she does not consider London a particularly bad environment for young people to live in, but at the same time she is not convinced that London has anything special to offer young people. Indeed, she might want to think twice before advising young people to come to London to seek work. She reckons that young people like herself could do with a lot more help and that there is a need for more counselling facilities for young people in London.

One of the things that Anna Mary would miss most if she were to leave London is her membership of London Central YMCA, where she spends quite a lot of her free time. Although she has been without work for much of the past year, Anna Mary has not found her leisure time dragging heavily. She is the sort of person who finds it important to be enjoying herself and the YMCA has helped her to do this. She takes an active part in sport and also enjoys watching others engaging in sport while she sits around as a spectator. Her three particular sports are badminton, squash and swimming; she has also recently taken up yoga. She finds the YMCA's lounge area and coffee bar a helpful place to relax and to meet friends.

Anna Mary does not feel that being unemployed is half as bad as some people would make out. Between them her boy friend and her father have cushioned the financial hardship of unemployment, while her membership of London Central YMCA has helped to cushion the isolation and social hardship of unemployment. All this has helped to colour Anna Mary's attitude towards work. She says that she is much happier being unemployed than working in a job she might dislike. Although money plays an important part in her life, she says that she would never go out and get a job just for the sake of the extra income. She sees no point in working just for the pay packet at the end of the week; Anna Mary feels that she needs and deserves much more job satisfaction than that. She has really set her heart on being a professional model. If she could find the right opening here, she says that she would be really ambitious and hard working, but while she goes on looking for the right job, Anna Mary feels no real reason to settle for something less satisfactory.

Anna Mary tries to be an open and honest person. She tries to admit the truth to herself and to other people. Although what other people think about her matters to her a great deal, Anna Mary does not try to win the good opinion of others by pretending that she is a better person than she really is. She is sufficiently mature and secure in her disposition not to need to tell lies about herself. For example, she does not pretend that she has never been guilty of taking things that do not belong to her. She is willing to admit that sometimes she will break the law if she feels that she is going to be able to get away with it. The kind of things that she reckons that it is alright to try to get away with are travelling on a crowded bus without paying her fare, or failing to declare some of her earned income to the tax people.

Another indication of her attitude towards the law is the way she evaluates motoring laws. Anna Mary takes a hard line against drinking and driving. She feels that the law is totally right on this point and ought to be firmly upheld. She also agrees with the way in which the law enforces speed restrictions, but she does not feel as strongly about this as about drinking and driving. On the other hand, she sees much less point in many of the regulations about parking.

Anna Mary likes to think of herself as really quite a self sufficient kind of person. She has certainly not allowed unemployment to erode her self-confidence and her ability to cope with life. She says that she finds life really worth living and that she does not need a job to give her a sense of purpose or a sense of value to her life.

The fact that Anna Mary does not worry much about being unemployed is characteristic of her whole approach to life. She does not usually let things play on her mind and worry her. For example, she is not the kind of person to worry about her relationships with other people or about her sex life. She does not generally worry about her health. She is not anxious about the problems of growing old or about the strains and stresses of modern life.

There are some occasions when Anna Mary feels lonely and depressed and finds herself longing for people to turn to for affection and advice. She says that she does not often need to talk to someone about her problems, but when she does feel this need she realises just how isolated she can be. Although she values her friends highly, Anna Mary does not tend to build up the kind of friendships that encourage deep talking and trust. She has never turned to professionals for help and she is quite convinced that she would never be willing to do so. Anna Mary feels able to stand on her own feet and her confidence seems well placed.

Anna Mary shows up in the statistics as one of the unemployed young people in the London area. However, her reactions to being out of work have emerged as quite different from the stereotype of unemployed young people. Anna Mary may well find herself unemployed for quite a period to come, especially if she persists in her ambition to find work only in a modelling career, but she faces this prospect with equanimity. She is quite content with her present way of life and sees no fundamental need to change it.

JOSEF

Both of Josef's parents were born in Poland. Their families moved out during the Second World War and established a new life for themselves in England. Josef himself was born in England as a first generation citizen. His parents had, however, been intent upon preserving something of their national identity through the way in which they brought up their son.

Josef grew up in one of the poorer outskirts of London, about fifteen miles from the city centre. He attended the local comprehensive school and really hated it. He left school at the age of sixteen. That was just over a year ago, and since then Josef has been out of work. He says that he has no academic qualifications and no particular skills or aptitudes that suit him for any particular kind of work.

Although, at times, Josef makes the pretence of looking for work, he prefers to say that he is unemployed because of ill health. Josef's health problem is a psychological one. At home he has grown up in a very protective environment. His parents kept themselves very much to themselves and Josef had little opportunity to mix with other children. At school he made very few friends; he became withdrawn, aloof and isolated. Now he is frightened of going out and finding a job in case the experience of school repeats itself all over again. He continues to live at home with both of his parents.

Josef is beginning to formulate quite deep seated negative attitudes towards work. He says that he does not see any intrinsic value in work itself. He sees no point in hard work, if it is possible to get by without it. The only reason he can see for going to work is the money he could earn. But even then he does not feel that this is a very compelling argument. At the moment he has enough to live on without going to work. His parents are quite generous to him, and has been able to draw some state benefits. In fact, he says that he would much rather live on social security than get a job he did not like or which he felt uncomfortable doing.

On the whole, Josef holds a very poor view of contemporary British society; he says that he does not see much of a future for Britain at all. To quote just a few examples of his pessimistic view of life in England today, Josef reckons that the crime rate is rising, that the educational standard of schools is declining and that the efficiency of the health service is deteriorating. Having said what he thinks is wrong with life in Britain today, Josef has no remedy to improve things for the future. Certainly he has no faith in politics or in politicians being able to change the situation. As far as he can see, it makes absolutely no difference which political party is in power.

When it comes to an analysis of his views on specific political issues, Josef reveals a very ill thought through set of opinions. He holds a right wing view about private medicine and a left wing view about private education. He holds a right wing view about trade unions and a left wing view about the nationalisation of industry. On international issues, Josef tends to favour the Common Market and he believes that immigration into Britain should be restricted.

Josef's social values are indicated by his attitude towards the pay claims of different groups of workers. Coming from a working class background himself, Josef is a consistent champion of the rights of the manual worker. The two groups of workers which he instinctively feels are undervalued and underpaid for the job they do are the car workers and the miners. He also supports, although less strongly, the case of nurses. On the other hand, Josef has no time for the professional classes. He feels that people tend to over-value professional groups like doctors and clergy at the expense of the working man.

Josef regards himself as a very law-abiding citizen. Thus, he argues that he would never try to get away with travelling on public transport without first buying a ticket. He says that he would never try to bring an extra bottle of spirits through the customs, or knowingly attempt to defraud the Inland Revenue. He believes that motoring laws should be strictly obeyed, right from parking restrictions, through speed limits, to not drinking and driving.

Josef's conservative attitude towards the law is also largely reflected in his attitude towards moral questions. To begin with, Josef takes a very conservative approach towards drugs and alcohol. He disagrees very strongly with the use not only of hard drugs like heroin, but also softer drugs like marijuana. Similarly, he argues very strongly that it is wrong to become drunk.

Josef also adopts a conservative attitude towards issues like abortion and euthanasia. He objects quite strongly to the practice of euthanasia and very strongly to the practice of abortion. He feels that nowadays society is making it too easy for women to have an abortion. In a similar way, Josef finds himself being critical of contemporary moral trends over a whole range of issues, including the divorce rate, the availability of pornography and the amount of violence screened on television.

On the ethics of sexual practices, however, Josef has adopted a much more liberal point of view, and one which seems quite inconsistent with his general moral and social stance. Josef has no hesitation in supporting the notion of sexual relationships outside marriage. He is totally in favour of the practice of contraception. To complete the picture, he gives his total approval to homosexual practices as well.

Although his home background is nominally Roman Catholic, Josef has long since lost any real contact with the church. He no longer regards himself as a Roman Catholic and it is now getting on for five years since he last attended a place of worship. He has not opened a copy of the bible since leaving school. His attitude towards religion has really become quite hostile. He feels that the bible and the church are quite irrelevant for life today. The clergy whom he has met have all singularly failed to impress him. He has never wanted to confide in the clergy or to turn to them for advice. Like the church itself, he feels that the clergy are irrelevant in today's world. If he had his own way, Josef would ban religious education from its place in schools.

In spite of his pronounced and hostile attitude towards the church and towards religion in general, Josef would still want to regard himself as a believer and call himself a Christian. After all, he says that he believes in God and accepts belief in Jesus Christ as the Son of God. Moreover, he frequently turns to God in prayer in order to seek help with the problems of living. What more, he asks, can be required of him before he can call himself a Christian?

Josef is insecure and unsure of himself in the company of

others. He possesses quite a degree of insight into the cause of this problem, but so far he has not made a real effort to overcome it. The problem is that he does not know where to start. Josef is not reluctant to face the truth about himself, but, having faced it, he is far from sure what to do about it. All told, Josef has a very low opinion of himself. He does not feel he is worth much as a person. He does not expect other people to like him and so he expends very little effort to make himself likeable.

As a result of his deep seated personal insecurity, Josef often finds himself consumed with all sorts of worries and anxieties. He worries a great deal about his personal health; sometimes he convinces himself that he is incurably ill. He is anxious about the risks of failing to cope with life; sometimes he convinces himself that he is on the verge of a nervous breakdown. He worries a great deal about his relationships with other people. He is especially anxious about his inability to establish a satisfactory or lasting relationship with girls; sometimes he convinces himself that he will never have a satisfactory sex life.

Josef also projects some of his insecurities and anxieties away from his own personal life onto the wider world around him. He says that he worries a great deal about the world situation. He is anxious about the risks to his personal survival posed by the threats of environmental pollution or by the threats of a nuclear holocaust. Sometimes he convinces himself that the world is on the edge of the third world war.

Given all this worry, anxiety and fear, Josef feels that he derives very little from life. He is living without any sense of purpose or achievement. He says that he frequently feels extremely depressed. Depression makes him lethargic and so he often feels that there is little point in going on living; often he finds himself entertaining suicidal thoughts. It is his threats of taking his own life which give him his ultimate power over his parents and so assures him of their unrelenting support and protection.

Josef says that he has no real friends. He is an extremely lonely young man who feels that no one knows him and that no one loves him. He longs for friendship more than anything else in the world, but has very little idea how to go about making friends. In spite of needing their support so much, Josef feels that his parents do not really understand his needs, and consequently he no longer finds it helpful to talk with them. In particular, he says that it is a waste of time trying to talk about his problems with his father.

Given the fact that Josef does not feel that he can talk with his parents, and his very real lack of close friends, to whom can he turn? Some time ago Josef was put in touch with a counsellor, and he has derived a great deal of help from this professional relationship. Through his regular contact with the counsellor, Josef has just begun to trust himself more than he had before. In some ways, the counsellor has begun to give Josef the confidence to take risks, but only marginal risks.

One of the most significant contributions the counsellor has so far made to Josef's life is the encouragement he was given to go out and to join a club of some sort. It is through this channel that Josef came to seek membership of London Central YMCA. Having had his confidence bolstered to the point of completing his application form, Josef had very high hopes of what the club could do for him; he says, 'I hope London Central YMCA can help me get over my personal problems - socialising, making relationships with the opposite sex and overcome loneliness'.

Being unemployed since leaving school, Josef has found his leisure time hanging heavily. At home he says that he has nothing to do apart from sitting around listening to music all day long. He says that he finds television boring and hardly ever bothers to watch it. He says that, without friends, he has no reason to go out to the pub for a drink. At school he did not like games lessons; he has never learned to take part in sport or gained enjoyment from watching others engage in sport. Josef has longed for more things to do in his leisure time, but coming to London Central YMCA has been his first attempt to create a leisure time life for himself. If he can learn to make good use of the social and recreational facilities of London Central YMCA, Josef is likely to experience quite a transformation in his present way of life, but for this to be really possible the staff will need to become aware of his special needs and help him to overcome his initial difficulties in becoming established in the club.

PATRICIA

Patricia is a twenty-five year old Argentinian. She left her parents' home country after leaving school, and made her way to North America. She married her husband in the USA, but never really settled there. When her marriage broke up, she again decided to travel to another fresh start, and this time made her way for England. That was a little over two years ago. At first she tried to make a home for herself in Manchester, but found things there extremely difficult because of the shortage of job opportunities. After being without work for nearly eighteen months, she came to London, where she was more successful in finding work as a hotel receptionist. She says that the job she found is very poorly paid, but that she had no real choice in the matter. The good thing about the job is that it provides her with somewhere to live.

Patricia was surprised how difficult it was to find work and disliked intensely the long period of unemployment which she experienced. She says that she would rather do any form of work than be unemployed again, and it is not just a matter of the money. Patricia has come to believe that, without a job, she was missing out on so much more than just the money she might have earned.

Apart from her relief at no longer being unemployed, Patricia is not gaining much real satisfaction from her job. Although she likes the people she is working with, the job itself is routine and dull. She finds that she has no real motivation to make something worthwhile of this job. Consequently, she spends a lot of her time reading the job advertisements in the local newspaper in the hope that she might find something more interesting and better paid.

Patricia's unsettled background has taught her to take life as it comes, and not to worry over things. If she wanted, she could find quite a lot to be depressed about, but she does not want to do so. She says that there is no point in thinking about the past and worrying about the future. She has grown into the way of taking each day as it comes. Thus, Patricia never worries about her physical health or about her ability to cope with life. Although friendships and relationships are important to her and she takes them seriously, Patricia does not worry about her relationships. Similarly, although the need for a job to earn money is important to her, Patricia says that she has given up worrying about her work and about money matters as well. If she is in debt, she no longer worries about it.

Looking beyond her immediate horizons, Patricia says that no responsible person can look honestly at major world problems like pollution and the risks of nuclear war without experiencing a lot of anxiety. Patricia also feels concerned about the poverty of the Third World and the problems of refugees. Nearer to home, she feels that inflation and unemployment are beginning to take a serious and worrying toll on our way of life. Although she takes issues like these seriously, she also feels that worrying about them will not change the situation.

Her experience of life has taught Patricia to be quite self sufficient and to trust her own judgement. She is not troubled by self doubts. She agrees that it is helpful from time to time to talk things over with another person, but she feels that she needs to rely hardly at all on other people for the support of their affection or advice. When she needed help as a child, she says that she was lucky because both her mother and her father listened to her and tried to help her. Subsequently, she has had some very good friends with whom she has been able to talk. When her marriage was breaking up and she needed help, she came into contact with a clergyman, to whom she was very grateful at the time for his understanding and help. In spite of her feeling of self sufficiency, Patricia says that she would not hestitate to turn to a minister of religion again should she feel the need to do so.

Patricia believes that every individual must accept the ultimate responsibility for the way in which their lives turn out. It is no good blaming other people, circumstances, situations or chance. Her philosophy of life means that Patricia is determined to make the most of what comes her way. In spite of her unpromising circumstances, she still finds life really worth living and feels that she can detect a sense of purpose in it all. In spite of going through the breakdown of her marriage and experiencing all the problems of long-term unemployment, Patricia says that she has never lost hope or despaired. Life has never become so bad that she has questioned the point of living.

One of the ways in which Patricia has protected herself

from the problems life has pushed her way is by distancing herself from other people and detaching herself from their demands and pressures. Because of this, she can truthfully say that she does not feel jealous when other people appear to be getting a better deal from life than she is. Similarly, she does not believe that she ever takes advantage of other people in order to further her own ends.

Although Patricia says that she is by no means indifferent to what other people think of her, she is sufficiently secure in herself not to want to work at creating a good impression on first encounters. She admits openly and honestly to the socially undesirable features of her life. She is not ashamed to say that she has broken promises, told lies and taken things which did not belong to her. Similarly, she is not ashamed to let others know that she sometimes feels resentful when she does not get her own way.

As well as valuing her independence and trying to keep other people at an arm's length, Patricia says that it is very important to her to have some really close friends. She does not find it difficult to make friends and to build up quite deep relationhips with people who come to know her very well. Because of these relationships, she never feels really lonely. Friends are in fact so important to Patricia that she places them right at the top of her value system. In comparison, everything else takes second place.

After the priority of friends in her system of values, Patricia places the material resources which she will need in order to make a success of her new start in life in London. That is why making money is so important to her, and why she finds being in a low income job is so frustrating.

Although her financial situation severely limits the kind of things that she can do when not at work, Patricia is not the kind of person who finds it difficult to make good use of her leisure time. She does not dislike or easily tire of her own company. She enjoys reading and listening to music, but feels that television is often a waste of time. She does not buy a newspaper; she says that they are too expensive and that she can discover all she needs to know from listening to the radio and from talking with her friends. Until joining London Central YMCA Patricia did not go out very much either.

One of Patricia's major reasons for joining London Central YMCA was to meet people in order to widen her circle of friends in London. She hopes to make new friends by using both the sports facilities and the social facilities of the club. Her sporting interests include badminton, swimming, tennis and table tennis. Although Patricia complains that the membership fee of London Central YMCA seemed to be very high and deterred her from joining for a time, she says that after joining she discovered just what good value the YMCA represented. Patricia is grateful to the YMCA for helping her to feel at home in London and for extending her network of friends and interests.

Patricia's interest in the YMCA most certainly does not extend to embrace an appreciation of the association's religious dimensions. Patricia was brought up a Roman Catholic, but she has long since stopped describing herself as a Christian of any sort. It is now more than five years since she last attended a church, read the bible or prayed. After leaving her home country, she lost her faith and now regards herself as an agnostic. This does not mean that Patricia has lost her interest in religious matters, and she still retains the sense that there are dimensions of life beyond the here and now. She still sees the planet earth as being only a small part of a whole chain of being, and, more fundamentally, she still firmly believes in life after death; but she says that she can no longer go along with the Christian teaching about a God of love and about the divinity of Jesus Christ. Although she does not feel that with her present lack of belief she can honestly have anything to do with a church, Patricia still retains a very positive attitude towards the church. She believes that the churches and the bible have a lot of positive good to offer today's world, and she very much wants young people to be able to know about them through religious education in schools. In fact, Patricia seems rather to wish that she could rediscover a religious faith for herself, but she has no idea where to begin in order to do this.

Her Roman Catholic upbringing still casts a significant shadow over Patricia's attitude to moral issues, although she has grown to accept a more liberal approach to heterosexual ethics. She approves the practices of contraception and sex outside marriage, but that is where the liberalisation of her moral attitudes stop. Patricia does not accept abortion and euthanasia as morally right and she remains quite adamant that homosexuality is morally offensive. She is also conservative in her attitudes towards drugs and alcohol.

Her strict views on morality also encourage Patricia to adopt law-abiding attitudes. She disapproves of travelling on public transport without a ticket and of bringing an extra bottle of spirits though the customs without paying duty on it. She believes that tax returns should be filled in with complete honesty. She believes that parking restrictions and speed limits should be strictly obeyed and that it is very wrong to drink and drive. She does not approve of the sale of cigarettes to children under the legal age.

Patricia does not think that she has lived in England long enough to form any firm conviction about the British political system. The political views which she actually espouses tend to be right wing rather than left wing. On the industrial front, she neither supports the trade unions nor the principles of nationalisation. On the social front, she wishes to protect the future of independent schools and of fee-paying medical practice. On the international front, Patricia is much less clear where she stands politically speaking.

Although still relatively uncertain about the English political system, Patricia has not been slow to formulate a general reaction to the social climate in Britain. She feels that the British social climate leaves a lot to be desired. The kind of picture which she is assembling for herself is one of a society in which the crime rate is rising, the educational standard of schools is declining and the efficiency of the health service is being increasingly undermined. Looking around her at the moral climate of Britain, Patricia feels that pornography is far too readily available and that there is far too much violence shown on television. She feels that society's attitudes towards abortion and divorce are making both too readily available.

Although convinced that she now wants to stay in England, Patricia is far from sure what sort of future she can predict for herself here. However, the disappointments and vicissitudes of her own life have taught her not to let uncertainty about the future worry her too seriously.

TOM

Tom is a nineteen year old youth who was born in the
Greater London area of mixed Anglo-Indian parentage. Tom
left school at the age of sixteen without any O levels, and
trained to become a hairdresser. After qualifying, he
spent an unsuccessful year seeking an appointment, before
being offered a part-time job in a local ladies'
hairdressers. Tom is single. When his parents got
divorced a couple of years ago, he moved away from his
parental home and found a place of his own in a house
which he shares with a number of other people, about
twelve miles from the centre of London.

Tom is not deriving much pleasure from his new part-time
job. He feels that he was better off unemployed. It is not
that he dislikes hairdressing; he likes the work and he
says that he wants to make the most of his career and to
do well in it. He is unhappy in his present job because he
cannot get on well with the other members of staff. He
feels that, as the newest employee and as a part-timer at
that, the others leave him an unfair share of the boring
side of the work. If he were given the chance to decide
again, he would much rather draw unemployment benefit
than commit himself to a job he so dislikes.

In spite of his disenchantment with his job, Tom is not
generally discontented with his life as a whole. He says
that he is determined to get the most out of life and that
nothing and no-one is going to stand in his way. Tom
rarely allows himself to feel depressed. He rarely worries
about his ability to cope with life or about his real worth as
a person. He did not allow being unemployed for nearly a
year to really get him down. Tom is the kind of person
who will go on fighting the system, and who is determined
not to let the system beat him.

In many ways, Tom feels that he is well suited to life in
London. He likes being part of a crowded city and to have
lots of people around him. Loneliness is not an experience
at all familiar to Tom. He feels that he has enough friends
around him who know him quite well and to whom he can
turn for support when he needs it. However, generally
speaking, Tom regards himself as a quite self sufficient
young man. He does not often feel the need to turn to
others for affection or advice; he does not often feel the

need to talk about his problems with other people. Indeed, he has never found it helpful to talk things over with either of his parents or, for that matter, even with close friends.

Tom's independence and self sufficiency are also clearly reflected in his attitude towards what other people think of him. Tom expects other people to accept him as he is. Although he takes considerable trouble over his personal appearance, he has no desire to put on an act and to pretend that he is something better than he really is. He does not attach much importance to what other people really think of him.

Tom is not ashamed to admit that there have been times when he has broken his promise, told lies, or taken things that did not belong to him. Similarly, he is open about his uncharitable emotions and feelings. Sometimes he feels jealous of others when they seem to be getting on better than he is. Sometimes he feels resentment when he does not get his own way. Sometimes he has taken advantage of people.

By taking life as it comes, Tom does not often find himself worrying about things. To begin with, he says that he hardly ever worries about himself. He does not worry about his health, about growing old or about the risks of cancer. He does not doubt his ability to cope with life or question his worth as a person. Similarly, Tom hardly ever worries about his relationships with other people or about his sex life. Although he is unhappy with his work, he never worries about it. Against this apparently care-free backcloth, there is just one area that worries Tom a lot. He is extremely worried about money matters and about the debts he has accrued, first while being unemployed and then while being in a low income job.

Money plays a very central part in Tom's system of values. Although, at the present time, he does not really want to put himself out to get a better paid job or, indeed, particularly like the idea of working hard, Tom says that he finds it extremely important to have money in his pocket to spend on the things he wants. He believes that one of the things which is really important in life is to be able to have a good time and, after all, that costs money.

Tom's idea of having a good time is to be out and about with his friends. He is often to be found drinking with his

friends, engaging in team sports, or following his favourite
football team, whether they are playing away or at home,
again in the company of his friends. Tom says that his
friends are very important to him, in strong contrast to his
home and family who hardly matter to him at all.

When he is unable to be out with his friends, Tom soon
discovers that his leisure time drags heavily. When at
home, he watches television most of the time, or listens to
music. He does not take much of an interest in the
newspapers and never reads books. Tom needs to be part
of a crowd, and he quickly bores of his own company. He
says that he wishes that he had more things to do with his
leisure time, and that this was one of his main reasons for
joining London Central YMCA. Through the YMCA he
wants to meet people and to make friends, as well as to
make good use of the sports facilities.

Tom certainly did not choose to join the YMCA because of
its Christian foundation. As a child, Tom was never
brought up to believe in religion, and as a consequence he
has never given much thought to religious issues. When
pushed to state his religious beliefs, Tom regards himself
as an agnostic who neither knows, nor really cares,
whether or not there is a God. He says that he has no
firm views on who Jesus Christ is, or whether there is life
after death or not. He cannot see why these questions
should really matter to him anyway. It is now more than
five years since Tom last had any practical contact with
religion. During the past five years, he has neither
prayed, read the bible, nor attended a place of worship.
His lack of involvement in religion is not so much a
rejection of religious values as an ignorance of what they
really stand for and mean.

While religion plays no part in Tom's life, he says that he
gives a little more attention to politics, although not to the
point of becoming actively involved in politics. On closer
examination, his political enthusiasm is very largely
uninformed, and involves little more than being quite clear
about the party for which he would vote in an election.
Tom believes that the Labour party has all the answers,
while the other parties are rubbish. For an enthusiastic
supporter of the Labour party, all of Tom's views on
specific political issues are surprisingly right-wing. He
disagrees very strongly with the nationalisation of industry,

while supporting with equal vigour the preservation of private enterprise in education and medicine, through independent schools and fee-paying medical practice. Moreover, Tom does not support the trade unions. Just as he has never bothered to find out what the church, which he does not support, actually believes, so Tom appears never to have investigated what the Labour party, which he does support, believes in the political arena.

Tom is far from sure what to make of the world situation, apart from experiencing a general sort of unease with the way in which things are going. He feels that the dangers from pollution and the risks of nuclear war are all too close at hand, and that inflation is biting too hard into the world. On the other hand, he feels nothing about the plight of homelessness or the poverty of the Third World. In spite of his own recent and prolonged experience of unemployment, Tom says that the issues underlying unemployment are of no particular concern to him.

When invited to assess the value ascribed by society to a variety of different groups of workers, once again Tom dismisses the question as one about which he has never really thought and which he does not consider worth worrying himself about. He is not concerned whether doctors, policemen, miners, car workers or clergy are adequately paid for the job they do in society. The one group, however, about which he has views are the nurses. He clearly believes that nurses are indeed underpaid for the job they do, but even then he does not feel strongly about the matter.

In contrast to Tom's general lack of clarity regarding his religious beliefs and his political attitudes, are his clear views on moral issues. Tom claims that moral values are important to him, and he certainly gives the impression of having developed a consistent approach to moral questions. To begin with, he does not believe that the traditional inhibitions of sexual relationships have any relevance for today. He approves both sex outside marriage and homosexuality without question. He cannot see the point of arguments advanced to question the morality of contraception or abortion, although he is less certain about the ethics of euthanasia. On the issue of the morality of drugs and intoxicants, Tom wants to condone the use of alcohol and marijuana; if people wish to get high in that kind of way, he does not believe that anything should stand in their way, although he does draw the line firmly against the use of heroin.

Taking a deliberately liberal view on moral issues himself, Tom does not believe that British society has generally made enough progress in the liberalisation of its moral standards. Tom believes that society is still making it too difficult for people to obtain a divorce or to have an abortion. He also believes that there is still too much censorship on the availability of pornography in the shops and on the amount of violence that is permitted to be screened on television.

Not only does Tom express irritation with the moral standards traditionally imposed by society, he also adopts a more fundamental antagonism against the restrictions imposed by the law. For example, he regards all motoring laws as tiresome and useless irritations. He sees no point in obeying parking restrictions or speed limits. He does not even see the laws against drinking and driving as being necessary; he argues that there is nothing wrong in drinking and driving while under the influence of alcohol, providing you can get away with it. In a similar vein, Tom maintains that it is quite permissible to try to travel on public transport without paying a fare, or to bring an extra bottle of spirits through the customs without paying customs duty on it. He believes that the individual is entitled to evade income tax by failing to declare all earnings. He sees no reason why the sale of cigarettes should be denied to children.

At the end of the day, Tom remains angry with society, and he intends to have the last word in the only way in which the powerlessness of his situation makes it possible for him. He refuses to obey the authority of those whom he holds responsible for building a society which has failed to fulfill its promises of prosperity and employment to his generation.

144

Bibliography

Ackerman, J.H. and Vaeth, M.F., The relationship between unemployment and health. The Ohio State Medical Journal, 74, 639-641, 1978.

Aiken, M., Ferman, L.A. and Sheppard, H.L., Economic failure, alienation and extremism. The University of Michigan Press, Ann Arbor, 1968.

Anwar, M., Young people and the job market: a survey. Commission for Racial Equality, London, 1982.

Bakke, E.W., The unemployed man. Nisbett, London, 1933.

Bakke, E.W., Citizens without work. Yale University Press, New Haven, Conn., 1940.

Bakke, E.W., The unemployed worker. Yale University Press, New Haven, Conn., 1940.

Bakke, E.W., The Cycle of Adjustment to Unemployment. In N.W. Bell and E.F. Vogal (Eds). A modern introduction to the family. Free Press, New York, 1960.

Ball, C. and Ball, M., Fit for work? Youth, school and (un)employment. Chameleon, Richmond, 1979.

Banks, M.H. and Jackson, P.R., Unemployment and risk of minor psychiatric disorder in young people: cross-sectional and longitudinal evidence. Psychological Medicine, 12, 789-798, 1982.

Barnett, L., The effects of unemployment and underemployment on newly qualified teachers. Unpublished paper, Department of Social Psychology, London School of Economics, 1983.

Bates, C.A., Change in self-image of school leavers experiencing work, unemployment or full-time further education (FE). British Journal of Educational Psychology, 52, 264, 1982.

Beales, A.L. and Lambert, R.S., Memoirs of the unemployed. Gollancz, London, 1934.

Beatty, R.W., Supervisory behaviour related to job success and hard-core unemployment over a two-year period. Journal of Applied Psychology, 59, 38-42, 1974.

Beckmam, R.O., Mental perils of the unemployed. Occupations, 12, 28-35, 1933.

Berthoud, R., Unemployed professionals and executives. Policy Studies Institute, London, 1979.

Bloxham, S., Social behaviour of the young unemployed. British Journal of Educational Psychology, 52, 264-265, 1982.

Bond, M., Art on the dole. Youth in Society, 77, 18-19, 1983.

Bowser, S.W., Sherman, G. and Whisler, R.H., An action-research approach to central city unemployment. Journal of Vocational Behaviour, 4, 115-125, 1974.

Braginsky, D.D. and Braginsky, B.M., Surplus people: their lost faith in self and system. Psychology Today, 9, 68-72, 1975.

Breakwell, G., Harrison, B. and Propper, C., The psychological benefits of YOPs. New Society, 61, 494-5, 1982.

Brennan, M.E. and Lancashire, R., Association of childhood mortality with housing status and unemployment. Journal of Epidemiological Community Health, 32, 28-33, 1978.

Brenner, M.H., Mental illness and the economy. Harvard University Press, Cambridge, Mass., 1973.

Brenner, M.H., Unemployment, economic growth and mortality. The Lancet, (March) 672, 1979.

Brenner, M.H., Mortality and the national economy. A review, and the experience of England and Wales, 1936-1976. The Lancet, (September) 568-573, 1979.

Brenner, S. and Bartell, B., The psychological impact of unemployment: a structural analysis of cross-sectional data. Journal of Occupational Psychology, 56, 129-136, 1983.

British Association for Counselling, Proceedings of a national conference on counselling and the unemployed person. British Association for Counselling, Liverpool, 1981.

British Medical Journal, Hazards of unemployment. British Medical Journal, 282, 1179-1180, 1981.

British Medical Journal, Medical aspects of unemployment. British Medical Journal, 283, 1630-1631, 1981.

Brown, E., Grounded. Lion Paperbacks, Tring, 1982.

Burghes, L. and Field, F., The cost of unemployment. In F. Field (Ed.), The conscript army: a study of Britain's unemployed. Routledge and Kegan Paul, London, 1977.

Burghes, L. and Lister, R. (Ed.), Unemployment: who pays the price? Child Poverty Action Group, London, 1981.

Campbell, J., Balfour, H., Finlay, H. and Wilson, M., The role of the occupational health nurse in redundancy. Occupational Health Nursing, 21, 12-14, 1973.

Cashmore, E.E., No future: Youth and society. Heinemann, London, 1984.

Casson, M., Youth unemployment. Macmillan, London, 1979.

Cavan, R.S. and Ranck, K.H., The family and the depression: a study of one hundred Chicago families. The University of Chicago Press, Chicago, 1938.

Chappell, H., The family life of the unemployed. New Society, 62, 76-79, 1982.

Church Information Office, Work or what? A Christian examination of the employment crisis. Church Information Office Publishing, London, 1977.

Clague, E., Couper, W.J. and Bakke, E.W., After the shutdown. Institute of Human Relations, Yale University Press, New Haven, Conn., 1934.

Cobb, S. and Kasl, S.V., Termination: the consequences of job loss. Department of Health Education and Welfare, Cincinatti, Ohio, 1977.

Coffield, F., Borrill, C, and Marshall, S., How young people try to survive being unemployed. New Society, 64, 332-334, 1983.

Cohn, R.M., The effect of employment status change on self attitudes. Social Psychology, 41, 81-93, 1978.

Colledge, M., Unemployment and health. Community Health Council, North Tyneside, 1981.

Colledge, M. and Bartholomew, R., A study of long-term unemployed. Manpower Services Commission, London, 1980.

Colledge, M. and Bartholomew, R., The long-term unemployed: some new evidence. Department of Employment Gazette, 88, 9-12, 1980.

Collins, S.D. and Tibbitts, C., Research memorandum on social aspects of health in the depression. Social Science Research Council, Bulletin, 36, 1937.

Cox, S. and Golden, R., Down the road: unemployment and the right to work. Writers and Readers Publishing Co-operative, London, 1977.

Crick, B. (Ed.), Unemployment. Methuen, London, 1981.

Daniel, W.W., A national study of the unemployed. Political and Economic Planning, London, 1974.

Daniel, W.W., How the unemployed fare after they find new jobs. Policy Studies, 3, 246-260, 1983.

Daniel, W.W. and Stilgoe, E., Where are they now? A follow up study of the unemployed. Political and Economic Planning, London, 1977.

Davis, M., The lost generation: A portrait of American youth today. The Macmillan Company, New York, 1936.

Dennehy, C. and Sullivan, J., Poverty and unemployment in Liverpool. In Field F. (Ed.), The conscript army: a study of Britain's unemployed. Routledge and Kegan Paul, London, 1977.

Department of Employment, The young and out of work. Department of Employment Gazette, 86, 908-916, 1978.

Donovan, A. and Oddy, M., Psychological aspects of unemployment: an investigation into the emotional and social adjustment of school leavers. Journal of Adolescence, 5, 15-30, 1982.

Dunn, M., Psychiatric treatment of the effects of the depression: its possibilities and limitations. Mental Hygiene, 18, 279-286, 1934.

Economist Intelligence Unit, Coping with unemployment: the effects on the unemployed themselves. Economist Intelligence Unit, London, 1982.

Eisenberg, P. and Lazarsfeld, P.F., The psychological effects of unemployment. Psychological Bulletin, 35, 358-390, 1938.

Elderton, M. (Ed.), Case studies of unemployment. University of Pennsylvania Press, Philadelphia, 1931.

European Centre for Work and Society, Growing up without work: two case studies. Community Projects Foundation, London, 1983.

Eyer, J., Does unemployment cause death rate peak in each business cycle? International Journal of Health Services, 7, 625-662, 1977.

Fagin, L., Unemployment and health in families. DHSS, London, 1981.

Fagin, L. and Little, M., The forsaken families: the effects of unemployment on contemporary British life. Penguin, London, 1984.

Field, F. (Ed.), The conscript army: a study of Britain's unemployed. Routledge and Kegan Paul, London, 1977.

Fineman, S., A psychological model of stress and its application to managerial unemployment. Human Relations, 32, 323-345, 1979.

Fineman, S., White collar unemployment: impact and stress. John Wiley and Sons Ltd, Chichester, 1983.

Fineman, S., Potter, K.C. and Jacobs, M., Work and no work. British Association of Counselling, Liverpool, 1981.

Fisher, A., Psychiatric follow-up of long term industrial employees subsequent to plant closure. International Journal of Neuropsychology, 11, 267-275, 1965.

Fleming, D. and Lavercombe, S., Talking about unemployment with school leavers. British Journal of Guidance and Counselling, 10, 22-33, 1982.

148

Fraser, C., The social psychology of unemployment. In M.A. Jeeves (Ed.). Psychology Survey No. 3. George Allen and Unwin, London, 1980.

Friedlander, F. and Greenberg, S., Effect of job attitudes, training and organisation climate on performance of the hard-core unemployed. Journal of Applied Psychology, 55, 287-295, 1971.

Friend, A. and Metcalf, A., Slump city. Pluto Press, London, 1981.

Frith, S., Downtown: young people in a city centre. National Youth Bureau, Leicester, 1981.

Fryer, D., and Warr, P., Unemployment and cognitive difficulties. British Journal of Clinical Psychology, 23, 67-68, 1984.

Furnham, A., The Protestant work ethic and attitudes towards unemployment. Journal of Occupational Psychology, 55, 272-285, 1982.

Furnham, A., Attitudes towards the unemployed receiving social security benefits. Human Relations, 36, 135-150, 1983.

Garraty, J.A., Unemployment in History. Harper and Row, New York, 1978.

Ginsberg, S.W., What unemployment does to people: study in adjusting to crisis. American Journal of Psychiatry, 99, 439-446, 1942.

Goodchild, J.D. and Smith, E.E., The effects of unemployment as mediated by social status. Sociometry, 26, 287-293, 1963.

Gore, S., The effects of social support in moderating the health consequences of unemployment. Journal of Health and Social Behaviour, 19, 157-165, 1978.

Gould, T., Out of work: the experience. New Society, 17, 859-861, 1971.

Gould, T. and Kenyon, J., Stories from the dole queue. Temple Smith, London, 1972.

Gravelle, H.S.E., Hutchinson, G. and Stern, J., Mortality and unemployment: a critique of Brenner's time-series analysis. The Lancet, (September) 675-9, 1981.

Green, W., The Christian and unemployment. Mowbray, London, 1982.

Greenwood, W., Love on the dole: a tale of the two cities. Cape, London, 1933.

Gurney, R.M., The effects of unemployment on the psycho-social development of school leavers. Journal of Occupational Psychology, 53, 205-213, 1980.

Gurney, R.M., Does unemployment affect the self esteem of school leavers? Australian Journal of Psychology, 32, 175-182, 1980.

Gurney, R.M., Leaving school, facing unemployment, and making attributions about the causes of unemployment. Journal of Vocational Behaviour, 18, 79-91, 1981.

Gurney, R. and Taylor, K., Research on unemployment: defects, neglect and prospects. Bulletin of the British Psychological Society, 34, 349-352, 1981.

Hall, O.M., Attitudes and unemployment: A comparison of the opinions and attitudes of employed and unemployed men. Archives of Psychology, 165, 1-65, 1934.

Hakim, C., The social consequences of high unemployment. Journal of Social Policy, 11, 433-467, 1982.

Harrison, R., The demoralising experience of prolonged unemployment. Department of Employment Gazette, 84, 339-348, 1976.

Hartley, J.F., An investigation of the psychological aspects of managerial unemployment. Unpublished doctoral dissertation, University of Manchester, 1978.

Hartley, J.F., The impact of unemployment upon the self esteem of managers. Journal of Occupational Psychology, 53, 147-155, 1980.

Hartley, J.F., Psychological approaches to unemployment. Bulletin of the British Psychological Society, 33, 412-414, 1980.

Hartley, J.F., The personality of unemployed managers: myths and measurement. Personnel Review, 9, 3, 12-18, 1980.

Hayes, J. and Nutman, P., Understanding the unemployed: the psychological effects of unemployment. Tavistock Publications, London, 1981.

Hendry, L.E.O. and Raymond, M., Youth unemployment, leisure and life styles: some educational consideration. Scottish Educational Review, 15, 28-40, 1983.

Hepworth, S.J., Moderating factors of the psychological impact of unemployment. Journal of Occupational Psychology, 53, 139-145, 1980.

Herron, F., Labour market in crisis. Macmillan, London, 1975.

Hill, J., The social and psychological impact of unemployment: a pilot study. Tavistock Institute of Human Relations No. 2T:74, 1977.

Hill, J.M.M., The psychological impact of unemployment. New Society, 43, 118-120, 1978.

Hill, M.J., Harrison, R.M., Sargeant, A.V. and Talbot, V., Men out of work: a study of unemployment in three English towns. Cambridge University Press, Cambridge, 1973.

Hirsch, D. and Yates, T., Unemployment and crime: discipline or justice. Youthaid Bulletin, 9, 4-5, 1983.

Hirsch, S. and Farmer, R. (Eds), The suicide syndrome. Croom Helm, London, 1979.

Hyman, H.H., The effects of unemployment: a neglected problem in modern social research. In R.K. Merton, J.S. Coleman and P.H. Rossi (Eds), Qualitative and quantitative social research: Papers in honour of Paul F. Lazarsfeld. The Free Press, New York, 1979.

Israeli, N., Distress in the outlook of Lancashire and Scottish unemployed. Journal of Applied Psychology, 19, 67-69, 1935.

Jackson, P.R., Stafford, E.M., Bank, M.H. and Warr, P.B. Unemployment and psychological distress in young people: the moderating role of employment commitment. Journal of Applied Psychology, 68, 525-535, 1983.

Jahoda, M., The psychological meanings of unemployment. New Society, 49, 492-495, 1979.

Jahoda, M., The impact of unemployment in the 1930's and 1970's. Bulletin of the British Psychological Society, 32, 309-314, 1979.

Jahoda, M., Work, employment and unemployment. American Psychologist, 36, 184-191, 1981.

Jahoda, M., Employment and unemployment: a social-psychological analysis. Cambridge University Press, London, 1982.

Jahoda, M., Lazarsfeld, P.F. and Zeisel, H., Marienthal: the sociography of an unemployed community. Tavistock Press, London, (first published 1933) 1972.

James, P., Livingstone, R. and Walker, W., Sense of direction: exploring new prospects with unemployed young people. Community Aid Foundation, London, 1983.

Jewkes, J. and Winterbottom, A., Juvenile unemployment. Allen and Unwin, London, 1933.

Jones, M., Life on the dole. Davis Paynter, London, 1972.

Jordan, A.B., Pauper. Routledge and Kegan Paul, London, 1973.

Kasl, S.V., Mortality and the business cycle: some questions about research strategies when utilising macro-social and ecological data. American Journal of Public Health, 69, 784-788, 1979.

Kasl, S.V., Changes in mental health status associated with job loss and retirement. In J.E. Barret (Ed), Stress and mental disorders. Raven Press, New York, 1980.

Kasl, S. and Cobb, S., Blood pressure changes in men undergoing job loss: a preliminary report. Psychosomatic Medicine, 32, 19-38, 1970.

Kasl, S.V. and Cobb, S., Some physical and mental health effects of job loss. Pakistan Medical Forum, 6, 95-106, 1971.

Kasl, S., Cobb, S. and Gore, S., Changes in reported illness and illness behaviour related to termination of employment: a preliminary report. International Journal of Epidemiology, 1, 111-118, 1972.

Kasl, S.V., Gore, S. and Cobb, S., The experience of losing a job: reported changes in health, symptoms of illness behaviour. Psychosomatic Medicine, 37, 106-122, 1975.

Kaufman, H.G., Professionals in search of work: coping with the stress of job loss and underemployment. John Wiley and Sons Ltd, New York, 1982.

Kelvin, P., Peter Kelvin profiles the unemployed. Social Work Today, 12, 8-11, 1980.

Kelvin, P., Social psychology 2001: The social psychological bases and implications of structural unemployment. In R. Gilmore and S. Duck (Eds), The development of social psychology. Academic Press, London, 1980.

Kelvin, P., Work as a source of identity: the implications for unemployment. British Journal of Guidance and Counselling, 9, 2-11, 1981.

Kemp, F., Buttle, B., and Kemp, D., Coping with redundancy. Kogan Page, London, 1981.

Kemp, N.J. and Mercer, A., Unemployment, disability and rehabilitation centres and their effects on mental health. Journal of Occupational Psychology, 56, 37-48, 1983.

Komarovsky, M., The unemployed man and his family. Octagon Press, New York, 1940.

Kingsley, S., An investigation of personal constructs concerning unemployed older managers. Unpublished MSc dissertation, UWIST, 1976.

Lawton, A., Dying for a job. Youth in Society, 63, 7-8, 1982.

Lazarsfeld, P.F., An unemployed village. Character and Personality, 1, 147-151, 1932.

Lester, D., Suicide and unemployment. A re-examination. Archives of Environmental Health, 20, 277-278, 1970.

Little, C.B., Technical-professional unemployment: middle-class adaptability to personal crisis. Sociological Quarterly, 72, 262-274, 1976.

Lynd, R.S. and Lynd, H.M., Middletown in transition. Harcourt Brace and Co., New York, 1937.

Macrae, H., Emerson, S. ane Dickens, M., Narrowing alternatives: a study of young women and unemployment in Lewisham. Lewisham Women and Employment Project, London, 1981.

Makeham, P., Youth unemployment. Department of Employment, London 1980.

Manpower Services Commission, Young people and work. Manpower Services Commission, London, 1979.

Manpower Services Commission, A study of the long-term unemployed. Manpower Services Commission, London, 1980.

Marsden, D., and Duff, E., Workless: some unemployed men and their families. Penguin, Harmondsworth, 1975.

Marsh, L.C., Health and unemployment. Oxford University Press, Oxford, 1938.

Marshall, J.R. and Funch, D.P., Mental illness and the economy: a critique and partial replication. Journal of Health and Social Behaviour, 20, 282-289, 1979.

Martin, R. and Fryer, R.H., Redundancy and paternalist capitalism. Allen and Unwin, London, 1973.

Miles, I., Adaption to unemployment? University of Sussex, Brighton, 1983.

Miller, J., Situations vacant: the social consequences of unemployment in a Welsh town. Community Projects Foundation, London, 1982.

Millham, S., Bullock, R. and Hosie, K., Juvenile unemployment: a concept due for recycling? Adolescence, 1, 11-24, 1978.

Milson, F., Youth Unemployment. Epworth Review, 9, 1, 25-28, 1982.

Morton, N.W., Occupational abilities: a study of unemployed men. Oxford University Press, Toronto, 1935.

Moylan, S. and Davies, B., The disadvantages of the unemployed. Employment Gazette, 88, 830-832, 1980.

Murray, C., Youth unemployment: a social-pyschological study of disadvantaged 16-19 year olds. NFER, Windsor, 1978.

Norris, G.M., Unemployment, sub-employment and personal characteristics. Sociological Review, 26, 89-108 and 327-347, 1978.

O'Brien, G.E. and Kabanoff, B., Comparison of unemployed and employed workers on work values, locus of control, and health variables. Australian Psychologist, 14, 143-154, 1979.

Orwell, G., The road to Wigan pier. Penguin, Harmondsworth, 1937.

Pahl, R.E., Living without a job: how school-leavers see the future. New Society, 46, 259-262, 1978.

Pahl, R.E., Family, community and unemployment. New Society, 59, 91-93, 1982.

Pilgrim Trust, Men without work. Cambridge University Press, London, 1937.

Platt, S., Unemployment and parasuicide ('attempted suicide') in Edinburgh 1968-1982. Unemployment Unit Bulletin, 10, 4-5, 1983.

Pyke, F., The redundant worker: work, skill and security in an engineering city. University of Durham, Department of Sociology and Social Policy, Durham, 1982.

Ramsden, S. and Smee, C., The health of unemployed men: DHSS cohort study. Employment Gazette, 89, 397-401, 1981.

Rapoport, R., and Rapoport, R. N., Leisure and the family life cycle. Routledge and Kegan Paul, London, 1975.

Rees, T.L. and Atkinson, P. (Eds), Youth unemployment and state intervention. Routledge and Kegan Paul, London, 1982.

Roberts, K., Duggan, G. and Noble, M., Out-of-school youth in high unemployment areas: an empirical investigation. British Journal of Guidance and Counselling, 10, 1-10, 1982.

Rimmer, L. and Popay, J., Employment trends and the family. The Study Commission on the Family, London, 1982.

Roberts, K., Noble, M., and Duggan, J., Youth unemployment: an old problem or a new life-style? Leisure Studies, 1, 2, 171-182, 1982.

Rundquist, E.A., and Sletto, R.F., Personality in the depression: a study in the measurement of attitudes. University of Minnesota Press, Minneapolis, 1936.

Sainsbury, P., Suicide in London: An ecological study. Chapman and Hill, London, 1955.

Sathyvathi, K., Suicides among unemployed persons in Bangalore. Indian Journal of Social Work, 37, 385-92, 1977.

Sawdon, A. and Taylor, D., Youth unemployment: a background paper. Youthaid, London, 1980.

Schlozman, K.L. and Verba, S., The new unemployment: Does it hurt? Public Policy, 26, 333-358, 1978.

Schumacher, H.C., The depression and its effect on the mental health of the child. Mental Hygiene, 18, 287-293, 1934.

Selbourne, D., Wolverhampton on ice. New Society, 59, 94-96, 1982.

Seabrook, J., Unemployment. Quartet Books, London, 1982.

Shanthamani, V.S., Unemployment and neuroticism. Indian Journal of Social Work, 34, 43-45, 1973.

Shepherd, G., Psychological disorder and unemployment. Bulletin of the British Psychological Society, 34, 345-348, 1981.

Shlionsky, H., Preu, P.W. and Rose, M., Clinical observations on the reactions of a group of transients to unemployment. Journal of Social Pyschology, 8, 73-86, 1937.

Showler, B. and Sinfield, A. (Eds), The workless state: studies in unemployment. Martin Robertson, London, 1981.

Sinfield, A., The long-term unemployed. OECD, Paris, 1968.

Sinfield, A., Poor and out of work in Shields. In P. Townsend (Ed), The concept of poverty. Heinemann, London, 1970.

Sinfield, A., What unemployment means. Martin Robertson, London, 1981.

Slote, A., Termination - The closing at Baker plant. Bobbs-Merril Co., Indianapolis, 1969.

Smart, R.G., Drinking problems among employed, unemployed and shift workers. Journal of Occupational Medicine, 21, 731-736, 1979.

Smith, M.A. and Simpkins, A.F., Unemployment and leisure: a review and some proposals for research. Centre for Leisure Studies, Salford, 1980.

South Glamorgan Council for Racial Equality, Unemployment in a multi-racial community: a survey of the unemployed in the inner city area of Butetown, Cardiff. South Glamorgan Council for Racial Equality, Cardiff, 1982.

Stafford, E.M., The impact of the Youth Opportunities Programme on young people's employment prospects and psychological well-being. British Journal of Guidance and Counselling, 10, 12-21, 1982.

Stafford, E.M., Jackson, P.R. and Banks, M.H., Employment, work involvement and mental health in less qualified young people. Journal of Occupational Psychology, 53, 291-304, 1980.

Stern, J., The relationship between unemployment, morbidity and mortality in Britain. Population Studies, 37, 61-74, 1983.

Stirling, A., Preparing school leavers for unemployment. Bulletin of the British Psychological Society, 35, 421-422, 1982.

Swerdloff, E.S., The effect of the depression on family life. The Family, 13, 310-314, 1933.

Swinburn, P., The psychological impact of unemployment on managers and professional staff. Journal of Occupational Psychology, 54, 47-64, 1981.

Tausky, C. and Piedmont, E.B., The meaning of work and unemployment. International Journal of Social Psychiatry, 14, 44-49, 1967.

Tiffany, D.W., Cowan, J.R. and Tiffany, P.M., The unemployed: a social-psychological portrait. Prentice-Hall, Englewood Cliffs, New Jersey, 1970.

Thomas, D., A town under the hammer. New Society, 66, 236-238, 1983.

Trew, K. and Kilpatrick, R., The Daily Life of the Unemployed. Queen's University, Psychology Department, Belfast, 1984.

Unemployment Unit, A dossier of despair. Unemployment Unit, London, 1982.

Walbran, B., MacMahon, B. and Bailey, A.E., Suicide and unemployment in Pennsylvania 1954-1961. Archives of Environmental Health, (10 January) 11-15, 1965.

Walker, T.W.A., Biding time, reflections of unemployed young people in Kirkcaldy. Community Projects Foundation, London, 1982.

Warr, P.B., A study of psychological well-being. British Journal of Psychology, 69, 111-121, 1978.

Warr, P.B., Unemployment and mental health. SSRC Newsletter, 48, 25-26, 1983.

Warr, P.B., Psychological aspects of employment and unemployment. Psychological Medicine, 12, 7-11. 1982.

Warr, P. B., Work, jobs and unemployment. Bulletin of the British Psychological Society, 36, 305-311, 1983.

Warr, P.B., Job loss, unemployment and psychological well-being. In E. van de Vliert and V. Allen (Eds). Role transitions. Plenum, New York, 1983.

Warr, P.B., Work and unemployment. In P.J.D. Drenth, H. Thierry, P.J. Willems and C.J. de Wolff (Eds). Handbook of work and organisation psychology. John Wiley, Chichester, 1983.

Warr, P.B. and Parry, G., Paid employment and women's psychological well-being. Psychological Bulletin, 91, 498-516, 1982.

Warr, P.B., Jackson, P.R. and Banks, M.H., Duration of unemployment and psychological well-being in young men and women. Current Psychological Research, 2, 207-214, 1982.

Warr, P.B. and Parry, G., Depressed mood in working class mothers with and without paid employment. Social Psychiatry, 17, 161-165, 1982.

Watt, D. and Klein, R. (Eds), Unemployment symposium. Political Quarterly, 52, No. 1, 1981.

Watts, A.G., The implications of school leaver unemployment for careers education in schools. Journal of Curriculum Studies, 10, 233-250, 1978.

Watts, A.G., Unemployment: implications for careers education. Hobsons Press for Careers Research and Advisory Council, Cambridge, 1982.

Watts, A.G., Education, unemployment and the future of work. Open University Press, Milton Keynes, 1983.

Wedderburn, D., White-collar redundancy. Cambridge University Press, Cambridge, 1964.

Wedderburn, D., Redundancy and the railwaymen. Cambridge University Press, Cambridge, 1965.

Wedderburn, D., Unemployment in the seventies. Listener, (12 August), 1971.

Williams, R.S., Morea, P.C. and Ives, J.M., The significance of work: an empirical study. Journal of Occupational Psychology, 48, 45-51, 1975.

Williamson, H., Chance would be a fine thing. National Youth Bureau, Leicester, 1981.

Winfield, I., Psychology and centres for the unemployed: challenge or chimera? Bulletin of the British Psychological Society, 34, 353-355, 1981.

Wood, S., Redundancy and stress. In D. Gowler and K. Legge (Eds). Managerial stress. Gower Press, Farnborough, 1975.

Woolston, H.B., The psychology of unemployment. Social Science Research, 19, 335-340, 1934.

Worswick, G.D. (Ed), The concept and measurement of involuntary unemployment. George Allen and Unwin, London, 1976.

Wright, H.R., The families of the unemployed in Chicago. Social Services Review, 8, 17-30, 1934.

Zawadski, B, and Lazarsfeld, P.F., The psychological consequences of unemployment, Journal of Social Psychology, 6, 224-251, 1935.

Appendices

Appendix 1 Correlation with unemployment

	Correlation With Unemployment
1. I listen to the radio or television news nearly every day	-.1029
3. Frequently I wish I could change my job	+.0496
4. I like living in England	-.0827
8. I take an active part in sport	-.0791
10. I often feel feel depressed	+.0987
12. I like the people I work with	-.0954
15. I believe that it is becoming too easy to obtain an abortion	-.0621
18. There is nothing wrong in selling cigarettes to children under the legal age	+.0407
19. I would never discuss my problems with a trained counsellor	-.0683
23. I am worried about my relationships with other people	+.0474
26. I believe that the crime rate is rising	-.0512
33. I think private schools should be abolished	+.0774
36. I think doctors are underpaid for the job they do	-.0826
37. Saving money is important to me	-.0474
41. I feel I am not worth much as a person	+.0865
46. I am worried that I cannot cope	+.0818
48. I think policemen are underpaid for the job they do	-.0819

Appendix 1 Correlation with unemployment (continued)

	Correlation With Unemployment
52. I have confidence in the policies of the Conservative party	-.0521
53. I am worried about my sex life	+.0778
54. I have sometimes considered taking my own life	+.1146
55. I am happy in my job	-.0626
56. I think the practice of homosexuality is wrong	-.0979
61. I think it is wrong to use marijuana	-.0618
62. I think the trade unions have too much power	-.0643
64. It is not wrong to travel without a ticket if you are not caught	+.0718
68. I often worry about my work	+.0419
69. I tend to be a lonely person	+.0512
71. I am worried that I might have a breakdown	+.0978
72. I often long for someone to turn to for advice	+.0627
73. I have found it helpful to talk about my problems with my father	-.0880
77. I believe in my horoscope	+.0421
78. My appearance is important to me	-.0427
79. I am concerned about the risk of nuclear war	-.0405
81. I read a newspaper nearly every day	-.0785
87. I think religious education should be taught in schools	-.0504

Appendix 1   Correlation with unemployment   (continued)

	Correlation With Unemployment
89. I often long for someone to turn to for affection	+.0866
90. I am worried about my debts	+.0685
94. I feel no one knows me	+.0843
95. I have found it helpful to talk about my problems with a trained counsellor	+.1205
96. I find life really worth living	-.0524
99. I think car workers are underpaid for the job they do	+.0553
102. My home and family are important to me	-.0795
103. I have never stolen anything in my life	-.0758
107. I would never discuss my problems with a minister of religion	-.0697
109. I believe in life after death	-.0409
110. I think that London has a lot more to offer the young person than other cities	-.0516
117. I believe in God	-.0588
120. I often watch sport in my leisure time	-.1364
121. I believe that it is becoming too easy to obtain a divorce	-.0858
126. I believe that there is too much violence on television	+.0586
132. I think suicide is a sin	-.0592
137. I would rather go on social security than get a job I don't like doing	+.1052
139. It is important for me to own my own house	-.1352

Appendix 2   Principal Factor solution, unrotated

	FACTOR ONE DEPRESSION			FACTOR TWO CONSERVATISM		
	Total Sample	Emp- loyed	Unemp- loyed	Total Sample	Emp- loyed	Unemp- loyed
1. I listen to the radio or television news nearly every day	-.16	-.14	-.12	+.11	+.05	+.15
3. Frequently I wish I could change my job	+.40	+.38	+.31	-.08	-.09	-.11
4. I like living in England	-.24	-.23	-.15	+.09	+.04	+.18
8. I take an active part in sport	-.22	-.16	-.26	+.08	+.04	+.09
10. I often feel feel depressed	+.59	+.56	+.70	+.11	+.12	+.01
12. I like the people I work with	-.34	-.38	-.18	+.08	+.12	+.12
15. I believe that it is becoming too easy to obtain an abortion	+.10	+.12	+.10	+.46	+.43	+.49
18. There is nothing wrong in selling cigarettes to children under the legal age	+.11	+.11	+.04	-.22	-.22	-.26
19. I would never discuss my problems with a trained counsellor	-.09	-.06	-.12	-.10	-.11	-.13
23. I am worried about my relationships with other people	+.60	+.61	+.59	+.06	+.03	+.00
26. I believe that the crime rate is rising	-.08	+.06	-.03	+.31	+.29	+.28
33. I think private schools should be abolished	+.22	+.21	+.11	-.24	-.20	-.35
36. I think doctors are underpaid for the job they do	-.12	-.15	+.04	+.21	+.16	+.25
37. Saving money is important to me	-.03	-.02	+.07	+.31	+.30	+.35
41. I feel I am not worth much as a person	+.50	+.52	+.48	+.02	-.01	+.05
46. I am worried that I cannot cope	+.66	+.68	+.73	+.14	+.09	+.12
48. I think policemen are underpaid for the job they do	-.11	-.13	+.05	+.30	+.29	+.27
52. I have confidence in the policies of the Conservative party	-.17	-.15	-.12	+.30	+.30	+.36
53. I am worried about my sex life	+.52	+.50	+.61	-.02	-.02	-.14

Appendix 2 Principal Factor solution, unrotated (continued)

	FACTOR ONE DEPRESSION			FACTOR TWO CONSERVATISM		
	Total Sample	Employed	Unemployed	Total Sample	Employed	Unemployed
54. I have sometimes considered taking my own life	+.54	+.52	+.53	-.02	+.00	-.09
55. I am happy in my job	-.45	-.47	-.33	+.14	+.14	+.16
56. I think the practice of homosexuality is wrong	+.02	+.08	-.07	+.36	+.32	+.45
61. I think it is wrong to use marijuana	-.02	-.02	+.04	+.48	+.48	+.43
62. I think the trade unions have too much power	-.17	-.17	-.05	+.35	+.32	+.41
64. It is not wrong to travel without a ticket if you are not caught	+.18	+.14	+.14	-.21	-.16	-.31
68. I often worry about my work	+.40	+.39	+.44	+.09	+.02	+.14
69. I tend to be a lonely person	+.64	+.62	+.70	-.05	-.01	+.03
71. I am worried that I might have a breakdown	+.70	+.67	+.72	+.12	+.13	+.01
72. I often long for someone to turn to for advice	+.61	+.60	+.67	+.24	+.25	+.06
73. I have found it helpful to talk about my problems with my father	-.11	-.07	-.05	+.26	+.27	+.24
77. I believe in my horoscope	+.20	+.15	+.31	+.23	+.28	+.12
78. My appearance is important to me	-.12	-.15	+.06	+.16	+.17	+.09
79. I am concerned about the risk of nuclear war	-.02	-.05	+.07	+.13	+.09	+.12
81. I read a newspaper nearly every day	-.21	-.16	-.29	+.07	+.02	+.15
87. I think religious education should be taught in schools	-.05	-.09	+.09	+.45	+.40	+.55
89. I often long for someone to turn to for affection	+.36	+.37	+.38	+.16	+.19	+.04
90. I am worried about my debts	+.26	+.28	+.20	+.09	+.13	+.00

Appendix 2   Principal Factor solution, unrotated   (continued)

	FACTOR ONE DEPRESSION			FACTOR TWO CONSERVATISM		
	Total Sample	Emp-loyed	Unemp-loyed	Total Sample	Emp-loyed	Unemp-loyed
94. I feel no one knows me	+.51	+.53	+.47	-.03	-.03	-.13
95. I have found it helpful to talk about my problems with a trained counsellor	+.27	+.28	+.21	+.29	+.32	+.29
96. I find life really worth living	-.51	-.51	-.49	+.10	+.13	+.13
99. I think car workers are underpaid for the job they do	+.25	+.22	+.23	-.04	-.01	-.13
102. My home and family are important to me	-.20	-.17	-.17	+.28	+.31	+.24
103. I have never stolen anything in my life	-.09	-.10	-.04	+.19	+.21	+.14
107. I would never discuss my problems with a minister of religion	-.06	-.07	-.01	-.31	-.33	-.34
109. I believe in life after death	+.02	-.01	+.10	+.44	+.42	+.47
110. I think that London has a lot more to offer the young person than other cities	-.09	-.12	+.01	+.02	-.02	+.01
117. I believe in God	+.01	-.01	+.12	+.59	+.61	+.59
120. I often watch sport in my leisure time	-.05	-.13	-.08	+.15	+.11	+.14
121. I believe that it is becoming too easy to obtain a divorce	+.04	+.05	+.07	+.43	+.40	+.48
126. I believe that there is too much violence on television	+.12	+.08	+.18	+.25	+.26	+.31
132. I think suicide is a sin	+.00	+.00	+.03	+.43	+.42	+.47
137. I would rather go on social security than get a job I don't like doing	+.20	+.17	+.15	-.23	-.20	-.33
139. It is important for me to own my own house	-.19	-.13	+.01	+.24	+.17	+.27
EIGENVALUES	5.27	5.28	5.44	3.37	3.19	3.89
% VARIANCE	26.7	26.7	22.5	17.0	15.9	16.1

Index